THE SHOW BOAT COOKBOOK

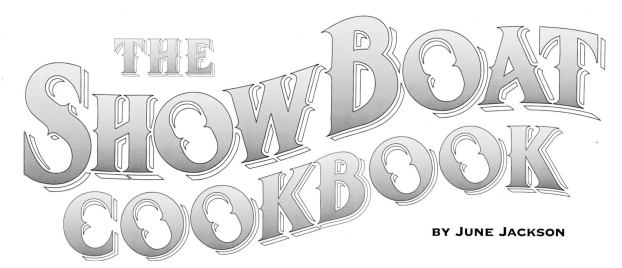

THE SHOW BOAT COOKBOOK

BY JUNE JACKSON

History of Show Boat
contributed by
Dennis Kucherawy

LEFT, The arrival of the *Cotton Blossom* at the Natchez levee, with the *Show Boat* Company.

JUDD PUBLISHING
UNITED PUBLISHERS GROUP
NORWALK, CONNECTICUT

Acknowledgements

First, thanks goes to Lynda Friendly, Executive Vice-President of Livent Inc., and to Theodore Chapin, President and Executive Director of Rodgers and Hammerstein. They, after all, said "yes" to the idea of the cookbook. Their cooperative spirit and enthusiastic approval gave first life to the project. And to Dennis Kucherawy, Vice-President–Communications of Livent Inc., for the history of *Show Boat*.

Much appreciation goes to Lou and Ralph Davidson, who gave us use of their home for the photographic sessions. Their daughter Mary Elizabeth contributed the edible pansies from the window box of her playhouse. Their other daughter, Sydney, was on hand for moral support.

Professional thanks goes to the following people who shared historical material, recipes and food thoughts: Dr. and Mrs. Thomas Gandy—Natchez, Mississippi; Stephanie Howard—Natchez Convention and Visitor Bureau; Liza Sharp—owner, Liza's Contemporary Cuisine, Natchez; Doris Ann Benoit—Monmouth Plantation, Natchez, Mississippi; Juanita Love—Chef, Monmouth Plantation, Natchez; Gertrude Payne—Chef, Carriage House Restaurant, Natchez; Paul Wayland-Smith—Executive Chef, The Delta Queen Steamboat Co., New Orleans, Louisiana; Lucette Brehm—Public Relations, The Delta Queen Steamboat Co., New Orleans; Stephen Harrison—Curator, Decorative Arts, Louisiana State Museum, New Orleans; Mrs. Russell Long— Board Member, Louisiana State Museum, New Orleans; Gene Slivka—Curator, Rosedown Plantation, St. Francisville, Louisiana; Staff Members—U.S. National Park Service, Oakley Plantation, St. Francisville, Louisiana.

Personal thanks goes to many people who added to my research, discussions and enjoyment of this project. These friends, family members and I have relished cooking and eating together and talking about the process all the while: My aunt, Grace Baur; Judy Bowles; Mary Connolly; Marilou Dennis; Pattie Gay; Beth Gibbens; Cathie Gill; Sandra Grace; Sam Hanna; Rue, Nancy and Sallie Judd; Dorothy Kidder; June Libin; Evelyn Pope; Carol Ravenal; my parents, Kathryn and Ross Reynolds; Pat Schieffer; Paul St. Martin; Ethelynn Stuckey and Eleanor Williamson Hatfield.—*June Jackson*

LEFT, "Can't Help Lovin' Dat Man," with *(left to right)* Gretha Boston as Queenie, Michel Bell as Joe, Lonette McKee as Julie, and Rebecca Luker as Magnolia.

Copyright © 1996 by Livent, Inc.

Text and recipes by June Jackson

History of *Show Boat* contributed
by Dennis Kucherawy.

How to Speak "River" pages 140, 141, 142
includes portions contributed by The Delta
Queen Steamboat Co. and used by permission
of The Delta Queen Steamboat Co.

Food photography by Lee Anderson

Historic photographs pages 8, 38–39, 51,
67, 76–77, 87, 99, 122–123, 140, 141, 142
©Joan W. Gandy and Thomas H. Gandy,
from the collection of Joan W. Gandy and
Thomas H. Gandy, Natchez, Mississippi

Production photography of *Show Boat* by
Catherine Ashmore. Additional photography by
Martha Swope, Michael Cooper and John Currid,
photography assistant.

Front Cover Design by Scott Thornley and Co., Inc.

Publication Design by Sicklesmith Design

This 1997 edition is published by
United Publishers Group and Judd Publishing Inc.,
by arrangement with Livent, Inc.

Printed and bound in Korea

**Library of Congress
Cataloging-in-Publication Data**

T/C

8 7 6 5 4 3 2 1

*Dedicated to Hayes and Scott,
who saw* Show Boat *with me
and who give me joy.*

Table of Contents

Foreword

My seeing *Show Boat* precipitated the idea for this souvenir cookbook. When I left the theatre, I wanted more of the *Show Boat* experience. Buying the cassette of the sound track extended the pleasure of having seen the musical, yet the characters continued to be alive for me.

The scene in "Queenie's Pantry" convinced me that Queenie cooked; reading Ferber's novel told me that Parthy made pickles and that a lady in the *Cotton Blossom* audience brought plum jelly and chocolate cake as a gift when the boat docked in her home town.

Having been born on the Mississippi River at Natchez and having grown up in the Delta, I found *Show Boat* so authentically descriptive of the historical South that a cookbook seemed to automatically emerge from the musical. The music, the sets and the food naturally go together.

At the outset, it was clear that the recipes should follow the route of the *Cotton Blossom* on her trip up and down the Mississippi, with stops (in the scope of the musical's story) at New Orleans, Natchez and Vicksburg and small towns in between.

Consequently, the book contains "river" food, victuals that were, and are today, common in the Mississippi Delta from the 1880s to the 1920s. Relying heavily on fresh vegetables, fruits and seafood—all bounty enjoyed by the entire social structure of the South—the recipes hopefully feed lovers of good food as well as good times, regardless of their positions in life. This book is for life's stevedores, boat captains, leading men and ladies, and good cooks everywhere.

Hopefully, this book will extend the reader's enjoyment of *Show Boat*. My goal will have been realized if the book is evocative of the marvelous production the playgoer thrilled to in the theatre.—*June Jackson*

LEFT, Franklin Street in Natchez in the 1870s was a busy area with many shops and the Pollock House hotel.

O n December 27, 1927, the course of musical theater history was changed forever with the Broadway premiere of the Jerome Kern and Oscar Hammerstein II epic, *Show Boat.* At a time when musical theater consisted of frothy entertainment with little substance, *Show Boat,* produced by the legendary impressario Florenz Ziegfeld, became the first musical play to combine serious, powerful themes with a rich Broadway score and a lavish, physical stage presentation in its sweeping romantic story of the lives of members of a theatrical family over four generations. It was innovative because its songs grew out of character and plot and because its mature subject matter—the social conditions and racial tensions of the South in the 1890s (including the issue of miscegenation), marital discord, self-destruction through alcoholism—did not follow the traditional pattern of musical comedy.

The musical is based on Edna Ferber's 1926 novel. Upon learning about the history of floating theaters on which acting companies lived and gave shows as they travelled the Mississippi River and its many tributaries, Ferber became enchanted with its literary possibilities.

Chapter One

HOW *SHOW BOAT* WAS LAUNCHED

LEFT, John McMartin *(standing on crate)* as Cap'n Andy selling tickets to the Natchez townsfolk (the *Show Boat* Ensemble) for that evening's performance of *The Parson's Bride*.

The first, modest version of a show boat is believed to have been a keelboat purchased by an Albany-born actor named Noah Ludlow in 1815 and christened *Noah's Ark.* However, an English actor, William Chapman Sr., built the first boat specifically designed as a show boat, called the *Floating Theatre,* and launched it in the summer of 1831. Essentially, it was a crude hut, 100 feet long and 14 feet wide, built on top of the hull of an ordinary, flat-bottom barge. The show boat's company consisted of Chapman, his wife and grown children who were all veterans of the London, New York and Philadelphia stage. Chapman would begin his season at Pittsburgh and float down the Mississippi River to New Orleans.

Show boats of the era, contrary to popular belief, were never self-powered, but were pushed by small twin-stacked steamboats that people actually called "tow boats." Townsfolk along the banks of the river would gather from miles around when they heard the distinctive, beckoning music of the show boat's calliope, a steam-driven pipe organ.

Life on the show boat was anything but glamorous, and often hard work. The Mississippi River, which traversed the spine of the USA, was a major means of transportation and commerce, and the busiest river in the country.

Although the Civil War brought the show boat era to an abrupt end, it began again in 1869 with the launching of the steamboat named the *Will S. Hayes.* By 1925, the show boats which had swarmed the river had, with a few isolated exceptions, disappeared.

Until recently, the only two remaining overnight paddlewheel steamboats still in existence, the *Delta Queen* and the *Mississippi Queen,* have carried tourists along the same river route the show boats used to travel. In 1995 a third, lavish new boat, the *American Queen,* was launched to recapture some of the lost magnificence of the era. However, authentic show boats—floating theaters pushed by small steamboats—remain a memory.

In 1924, Edna Ferber began researching show boats, then, in April 1925, joined the company and crew of the *James Adams Floating Theatre* in Bath, North Carolina, its first stop of a touring season that included the coastal tidewaters of Chesapeake Bay and the Albemarle and Pamlico Sounds. During her conversations with Charles Hunter and his wife, Beulah, who was the sister of the boat's owner, James Adams, Ferber learned that a typical show boat company included a romantic leading man and woman, ingenue and juvenile leads, a character team, a general business team, a villain, and a general utility man.

Her research completed, Ferber journeyed to Europe and, in the summer of 1925, in the small Basque village, St. Jean de Luz, she began writing the novel, *Show Boat*. She continued to write in Paris, and then completed the book in New York.

Show Boat was an immediate success. One of the book's admirers was composer Jerome Kern, who, before he had even finished reading the novel, wanted to adapt it into a musical.

In her 1940 autobiography, titled *A Peculiar Treasure,* Ferber recalled their meeting at a Broadway opening night that she attended with writer Alexander Woollcott, one of the famed members of the Algonquin Round Table. When Kern spotted Woollcott in the crowd, Kern went up to him and said, "'Look, Aleck, I hear you are a friend of Edna Ferber. I wonder if you'll kind of fix it for me to meet her. I want to talk to her about letting me make a musical from her *Show Boat*. Can you arrange an introduction or a meeting or something?'

"Mr. Woollcott, with a dreadful relish for the dramatic plum which had thus fallen into his lap (if any), said musingly, 'M-m-m, well, I think I can arrange it if I play my cards right.'

"'Thanks,' said Kern. 'Thanks awfully, Aleck, I'll be—'

"Woollcott now raised his voice to a bellow: 'Ferber! Hi,

RIGHT, *The Parson's Bride,* a melodrama of love and evil performed by the actors on the *Cotton Blossom*, with *(left to right)* Joel Blum as Frank, Rebecca Luker as Magnolia, Michael O'Carroll as the Backwoodsman and the *Show Boat* Company.

Ferber! Come over here a minute.' Then, 'This is Jerome Kern. Edna Ferber.' It was done."

Kern quickly recruited Oscar Hammerstein II to write the lyrics and book for the musical, meeting the challenges posed by Ferber's epic story that spanned forty dynamic years in American history. The story dealt, in part, with racial intermarriage, an issue never portrayed on the musical stage before. The plot also depicted sadness and suffering. How would audiences, accustomed to happy endings, respond?

The plot tells the story of the *Cotton Blossom,* a floating theater that plied the Mississippi and Ohio Rivers a century ago, and its owner, the jolly and generous Cap'n Andy Hawks; his domineering wife, Parthy; their lovely and innocent daughter, Magnolia, who falls in love with Gaylord Ravenal, a dashing riverboat gambler who joins the show boat troupe as an actor; and the tragically fated Julie, a victim of the oppressive miscegenation laws of the period.

Show Boat's first scene takes place on the levee at Natchez, Mississippi in the late 1880s, where the *Cotton Blossom* is moored, ready for that night's performance. Julie LaVerne, the romantic leading lady of the show boat company, and Steve, the romantic leading man, are happily married. However, Pete, the "river rat" who is the engineer of the *Cotton Blossom,* is infatuated with Julie and attempts to give her unwelcome gifts. Steve warns Pete to keep away from his wife. When Pete threatens revenge, Cap'n Andy fires him. In retaliation, Pete informs the local sheriff that Julie is of mixed race—one parent was white and the other was black. The fact that she is married to a white man, a criminal offence in Mississippi, forces Julie and Steve to leave the show boat. Magnolia is most distressed as she adores Julie.

Meanwhile, a handsome riverboat gambler, Gaylord Ravenal, who was drawn to the show boat by the sound of a piano being played on board, has met Magnolia and become immediately attracted to her. As he has been warned by the sheriff to leave town within 24 hours because of a crime in his past, Ravenal seeks passage on the *Cotton Blossom.* Cap'n Andy grants his request, but then presses him into service as the romantic leading man. Magnolia becomes the romantic leading lady and soon the on-stage romancing becomes real.

Parthy does not approve of Ravenal. Cap'n Andy dismisses her protests and gives his blessings for Magnolia and Ravenal to marry. The Ravenals prosper through Ravenal's gambling and move to Chicago following the birth of their daughter, Kim. A decade passes. Although Magnolia is still in love with Ravenal, he, down on his luck, decides to abandon her and Kim. He believes that Magnolia will return to her parents on the *Cotton Blossom.* Ellie and Frank, the former character team of the *Cotton Blossom* and now a prosperous vaudeville pair, find Magnolia in a shabby boarding house with very little money. They try to get her a job at the Trocadero Club where they are opening a new act. They are unaware that the featured singer at the club is Julie, who accidentally hears Magnolia audition for the manager. She sacrifices her own job to give Magnolia a break. Magnolia, during her singing debut on New Year's Eve, is jeered by the audience. But, it so happens that her father, Cap'n Andy, is part of the jovial crowd. He came to Chicago to find her, Ravenal and Kim. Cap'n Andy encourages Magnolia to continue her performance and persuades the crowd to listen to her. Magnolia finishes her act in a blaze of glory.

Twenty-seven years later, Cap'n Andy and Ravenal are on the upper deck of the *Cotton Blossom,* listening to a radio broadcast by Magnolia, who has since retired from a celebrated musical comedy career. Cap'n Andy has invited Ravenal to visit and

RIGHT, John McMartin *(left)* as Cap'n Andy performs "Cap'n Andy's Ballyhoo" with the *Show Boat* Ensemble.

convinces him to stay to see his wife and daughter, who are due to also visit the *Cotton Blossom.* While reluctant to face Magnolia again, Ravenal is most anxious to see Kim, now a young woman. Magnolia and Kim arrive. When Magnolia and Ravenal see each other, they are reunited and realize how deep and everlasting their love for each other remains, as Ravenal sings, "You taught me to see one truth forever true. You are love."

❦   ❦   ❦

Enraptured by the score's sweeping melodies and songs, including "Ol' Man River," "Can't Help Lovin' Dat Man," "You Are Love," "Why Do I Love You?," "Only Make Believe," and "Bill," and enveloped by the story's passionate drama, audiences fell in love with the musical. Brooks Atkinson of *The New York Times* called it "one of those epochal works about which garrulous old men gabble for twenty-five years after the scenery has rattled off to the store-house."

According to musical theater historian, Miles Kreuger, *Show Boat* was the turning point in the development of the genre. "The history of the American musical theater, quite simply, is divided into two eras," he wrote in 1988, "everything before *Show Boat,* and everything after *Show Boat.* This seminal work revealed that a Broadway musical was free to embrace any kind of theme, however controversial, could deal with serious issues in a suitably mature fashion, could counterpoint light and cheerful scenes with those of human anguish, and yet never need to sacrifice popularity and a memorable, tuneful score."

After a Broadway engagement at the Ziegfeld Theater lasting 572 performances, *Show Boat* opened five months later in London, England at the Theatre Royal Drury Lane on May 3, 1928, where it ran for 350 performances with the great Paul Robeson (who had been unavailable for the Broadway engagement) in the role of the stevedore, Joe, a part that would earn him international acclaim.

Following a silent movie adaptation in 1929 that combined elements of the novel and the musical, *Show Boat* returned to Broadway in 1932, opening at the Casino Theater on May 19 and running for 181 performances, playing to large crowds and standing ovations. Again, Brooks Atkinson hailed the musical, proclaiming, "After four-and-a-half years, it is still a thoroughbred; still the most beautifully blended musical show we have had in this country. Having developed logically out of a fragment of folklore, it is a work of art and a classic."

In 1936, Hollywood again beckoned, and a new adaptation of *Show Boat* was premiered on the silver screen starring Irene Dunne as Magnolia, Broadway's original Cap'n Andy, Charles Winninger, Helen Morgan re-creating her original performance as Julie, Paul Robeson as Joe and Hattie McDaniel as Queenie. The *New York Times* called the film, "The pleasantest kind of proof that it was not merely one of the best musical shows of the century, but that it contained the gossamer stuff for one of the finest musical films we have seen."

In 1946, *Show Boat* was revived on Broadway and returned to its original home, the Ziegfeld Theater, where it ran for 418 performances. In 1951, Hollywood filmed another screen adaptation, this time starring Kathryn Grayson as Magnolia, Howard Keel as Ravenal, Ava Gardner as Julie and William Warfield as Joe.

Throughout the years, producers continued to revive *Show Boat:* in 1966, at New York's Lincoln Center with Barbara Cook as Magnolia and Stephen Douglass as Ravenal; in 1971 in London with Cleo Laine as Julie; in 1982, at the Houston Grand Opera, a production that opened in New York in April 1983 at the Uris Theater, which is today known as the Gershwin Theatre; and again

in 1990 in London at the Palladium where it won the 1991 Olivier Award as "Best Revival."

The 1982 Houston Grand Opera production was the first to restore sections of the original script and score that had been cut, but had been rediscovered in the Rodgers and Hammerstein warehouse.

In 1988, EMI-Angel Records released John McGlinn's recording of *Show Boat* that attempted to present the musical's complete score as it was heard in 1927 and reinstated sections of the score that had been deleted during tryouts and productions over the years.

Livent Inc. restored Florenz Ziegfeld's original epic vision with its magnificent reexamination of *Show Boat*, directed by Harold Prince, that received its world premiere in October 1993 in Toronto, Ontario, Canada. The star-studded cast featured Robert Morse as Cap'n Andy, Elaine Stritch as Parthy, Lonette McKee as Julie, Rebecca Luker as Magnolia, Mark Jacoby as Ravenal, Michel Bell as Joe and Gretha Boston as Queenie. Featuring a company of 71 performers (twice the size of the cast of *The Phantom of the Opera*), a realistic riverboat setting by Tony Award-winning designer Eugene Lee, and more than 500 costumes designed by multi-Tony Award-winner Florence Klotz, this production was hailed by Frank Rich of *The New York Times* as "A seismic event in the American musical theater!"

Using the latest developments in computerization, automation, and other stage technologies that have been implemented in such contemporary blockbusters as *The Phantom of the Opera, Les Misérables,* and *Miss Saigon, Show Boat*'s creative team, led by producer Garth Drabinsky and Mr. Prince, rethought this classic and created a production of *Show Boat* for a new generation with scenes and production numbers that could not have been staged in the past.

The passage of time is central to Mr. Prince's vision, since previous productions of *Show Boat* never clearly established a historical context for the musical's tale. Unique to this production are two montages in the second act. The first illustrates the Ravenal family's trip from Natchez, Mississippi to Chicago in 1893. The second montage depicts the passage of time from 1900 to 1921 and features, as a central symbolic image, the wildly spinning, revolving door of Chicago's Palmer House Hotel.

In addition to lavish sets and opulent costumes, the passage of time is represented in Kern and Hammerstein's original score—

which Harold Prince calls the best ever written for a musical—as well as new orchestrations and dance music arrangements that trace the development of musical styles from work songs, spirituals and Victorian ballads to early Mississippi Delta blues, Dixieland, ragtime and jazz.

❦   ❦   ❦

Following *Show Boat*'s successful launch in Toronto, Livent decided to mount a second company to perform on Broadway where the musical's glorious legacy had begun 67 years earlier. The starring roles in this company would be played by many of the original Toronto performers, with the exception of John McMartin, who assumed the role of Cap'n Andy.

Given *Show Boat*'s status as one of the most beloved classics in American musical theater, and the fact that Harold Prince, one of Broadway's greatest directors was at the helm, the Broadway premiere of Livent's production of *Show Boat* on October 2, 1994, at the Gershwin Theatre was one of the most anticipated openings of the 1994-95 season. Mr. Prince is a legendary talent, responsible, as a director and/or producer, for such landmark productions as *West Side Story, Fiddler on the Roof, Cabaret, Evita,* and *Sweeney*

Todd among many others. The creative team was comprised of some of the world's finest theatrical talents including choreographer Susan Stroman, production designer Eugene Lee, costume designer Florence Klotz, lighting designer Richard Pilbrow, sound designer Martin Levan, production musical supervisor Jeffrey Huard, orchestrator William David Brohn and dance music arranger David Krane.

Such an array of talent coming together with producer Garth Drabinsky to collaborate on a re-creation of an American musical theater classic such as *Show Boat* deserved a gala premiere celebration worthy of such an historic Broadway event.

In keeping with the meticulous historical accuracy of this new production's direction and design, a festive opening night celebration was held at New York's opulent Plaza Hotel. It featured a glorious culinary feast of Southern foods and delicacies, representing the *Cotton Blossom*'s journey along the Mississippi River while reflecting the era and setting of the landmark musical. Two chefs from Natchez, Mississippi, one of the principal settings of *Show Boat*—Juanita Love of Monmouth Plantation and John-Martin Terranova of Liza's Contemporary Cuisine, under the coordination of Eliza Sharp, also from Liza's Contemporary

Cuisine—and another chef from New Orleans—Paul Wayland-Smith, executive chef on the *Delta Queen* paddlewheeler—joined forces with the Plaza Hotel's Executive Banquet Chef, Joseph Friel.

With the roar of the Gershwin Theatre audience's standing ovation still ringing in their ears, first nighters were greeted upon their arrival at the Plaza Hotel by Dixieland and swing music played by the Delta Queen Syncopators, who are regular performers on The Delta Queen Steamboat Co.'s paddlewheelers. Zydeco, jazz and blues musicians also performed. Castle and Pierpont, a New York design company, created the aura and ambience of a romantic, Southern evening by decking the Plaza Hotel's rooms with magnolias and gardenias. The Grand Ballroom was transformed into a Mississippi River setting, evocative of a Delta garden near a plantation, with smilax vines, Spanish moss, azaleas, dogwood blossoms, mosquito netting and festive, twinkling lights. A facade of the *Cotton Blossom Floating Theatre* towered over guests. Pastel parasols and sun bonnets surrounded by fresh flowers and ribbons festooned the table centerpieces. The mood was enhanced with large murals of historic riverboat scenes and evocative lighting.

Many of the recipes for the delicious food served that memorable evening are included throughout this book so that you can also experience a taste of the South inspired by *Show Boat*.

The morning following the opening, the airwaves and streets of New York were ablaze with the rave reviews. *Show Boat* had achieved unanimous critical acclaim. "The Great American Musical. Glorious and bold," heralded David Richards of *The New York Times*. Jack Kroll of *Newsweek* described it as "a big, big-hearted production" that "has been reincarnated on Broadway to remind us what a real show is."

Show Boat became the most honored show on Broadway during the 1994-95 season, winning five Tony Awards, including "Best Musical Revival" (tying the record for revivals set by the 1993-94 revival of *Carousel*), five Drama Desk Awards including "Outstanding Musical Production," and four Outer Critics' Circle Awards including "Outstanding Musical Revival."

After six decades, *Show Boat*'s romantic allure still captivates theatergoers.✍

RIGHT, The Curtain Call
with the *Show Boat* Company.

Chapter Two
THE PASSAGE OF TIME

Two prominent characteristics distinguish the Livent restoration of *Show Boat* from all the previous revivals and film adaptations: its emphasis on the passage of time and historical accuracy.

Show Boat takes place over a period of 40 years, from the Post-Reconstruction of the 1880s in the Deep South, to turn-of-the century Chicago in the North, through the exciting Roaring Twenties, the Jazz Age, to the eve of the Stock Market Crash and the Great Depression. This period was one of the most dramatic eras in American history, a time when the destiny of a land and its people was transformed forever.

Harold Prince's direction, the dance styles of Susan Stroman's choreography, Eugene Lee's production designs and Florence Klotz's costume designs all have contributed to the depiction of the passing of time. For example, Florence Klotz designed approximately 500 costumes that, through the changing silhouettes depict the evolution of fashion, from the curvy silhouettes of women in the 1880s created by corsettes and bustles to the flatter silhouette of the knee-length flapper dresses of the 1920s.

Historical authenticity is perhaps most prominent in Eugene Lee's set designs which create the illusion of a river onstage with

LEFT, Tammy Amerson as Kim *(dancing on car)* and the *Show Boat* Ensemble performing "Kim's Charleston."

the shimmering image of sunlight and water reflected on the weathered patina of the *Cotton Blossom* facade.

Upon entering the theater, one immediately notices the "show curtain," with its prominent daguerreotype image of "Natchez-Under-the-Hill" in the 1870s painted on the scrim, inspired by a photograph taken by American photographer, Henry C. Norman, celebrated for his historical photographs of post-Civil War life on the Mississippi. Norman's treasure trove of thousands of glass plates and celluloid negatives was purchased in 1961 by Thomas H. Gandy, a Natchez physician, who, with his wife, Joan Gandy, painstakingly cleaned, categorized and catalogued them. The negatives also included additional photographs taken by Henry Gurney and Earl Norman, Henry's son, that covered a period of almost a century.

The captivating images provide unique insight into life on the Mississippi River in the latter part of the 19th century, evoking memories of Natchez, which was a sophisticated town for its size. In the 1850s, only New York City boasted more millionaires!

A touring exhibition of 150 photographs from the Gandy Collection was seen in England at London's Barbican Centre and then travelled in October 1993 to the Ford Centre for the Performing

RIGHT, "Ol' Man River" performed by the Stevedores.

Arts in Toronto to coincide with the world premiere of Livent's production of *Show Boat.* The exhibition focused on such themes as Victorian Southerners at home and at play, Southern style and fashions, and scenes of the town streets and surrounding countryside. Included are images of river life—including the famous steamboats—portraits of the great antebellum Southern mansions built by the cotton culture, and photos depicting such major events as the arrival of President Taft by steamboat in 1909. Also displayed were portraits of store owners, passersby, and the first middle-class black families, representing what life was like from approximately 1870 to 1900 in the American South.

Eugene Lee's designs of the *Cotton Blossom* were further inspired by images in Dr. Richard Gillespie's book about the *James Adams Floating Theatre,* the same boat that Edna Ferber had visited on the Chesapeake when researching her original novel. For Eugene Lee, who has always lived near the water and has an affinity for boats, designing a production with two boats as major sets was a labour of love. "My intention from the beginning," he said, "was to be truthful to what the floating theaters were really like. The design comes from the actual truth of the period. The best work for this show has gone that way." ✍

LEFT, Act II, Second Montage depicting the passage of 21 years between 1900 and 1921, with the *Show Boat* Ensemble.

The *Natchez* approaches a landing where roustabouts wait to load and unload cargo.

Chapter Three

LANGUID BREAKFAST
ON THE FOREDECK

Chapter Three

When the steamboats were not laden with cargo, there was room on the foredeck to have a light, early morning meal. In our story, some of the Cotton Blossom *performers also meet here for a hurried conversation before rehearsals. When they have more time, they prefer to meet on the upper deck which has a better view, and relax while eating.*

BAYOU CREOLE EGGS WITH A DIFFERENCE

Most mornings on the Cotton Blossom, *there is no time for the cast and crew to ruminate or reminisce. Work must be done, and rehearsals begin early. Queenie, sometimes with Parthy's "encouragement," must prepare a Rise, Shine and Rehearse Breakfast that will "jump start" the actors, giving them the energy to sing, dance and act.*

YIELD: 8 to 10 servings

1 dozen eggs

1/2 cup whipping cream (2% or skim milk may be substituted)

2 tablespoons water

1/4 cup (1/2 stick) butter

1/4 cup fresh parsley, chopped

2 cloves garlic, chopped

1/4 cup green onions, chopped

1/4 cup red bell pepper, chopped

1/2 cup cheddar cheese, grated (optional)

1/2 teaspoon curry powder

Crack eggs into large bowl. Mix just enough to break yolks. Add cream and water. In large skillet, melt butter (or heat bacon drippings) and leave on medium heat until hot. Gently add beaten egg mixture and let "set" in pan about 1 minute. Stir lightly with spoon, just scrambling and add remaining ingredients. Cook on low heat until desired doneness is attained. Serve on warm platter. Surround with country bacon and sausage.

HORSERADISH SAUCE

The tang of the horseradish blends well with the strong flavor of the smoked fish.

Y I E L D : 1¹/2 cups

2 tablespoons butter

2 tablespoons flour

1¹/2 cups milk

¹/2 teaspoon salt

¹/2 teaspoon pepper

Paprika for garnish

Fresh chives, chopped

1 tablespoon prepared horseradish

1 tablespoon fresh parsley, chopped

In a saucepan, melt butter and add flour, stirring just until hot. Continue to stir for about 2 minutes. Slowly add the milk, whisking during entire addition. Cook for about 10 minutes, whisking or stirring constantly. Season to taste. Add horseradish and parsley and mix. Garnish with paprika and chives.

MORNING MIST EGGS ON THE COTTON BLOSSOM (with Horseradish Sauce)

In the early morning on the river, a low-lying fog hangs over the water. It clings to the trees and even to one's clothes, adding a romantic, haunted quality to the green landscape. By 10:00 am, it has either been blown off by the wind or burned off by the sun. Rising early enough to be a part of the scene gives one's day a special start that could lead anywhere. Riverboats carried various kinds of fresh fish and seafood for their passengers' dining pleasure; also popular were smoked and salted fish, such as trout and salmon.

Y I E L D : 4 large servings or 6 to 8 smaller servings

8 poached eggs

8 smoked trout or salmon fillets, 3 ounces each

or one pound boiled shrimp, shelled and deveined

Salt and pepper to taste

2 tablespoons fresh chives, chopped, for garnish

8 lemon slices, for garnish

1¹/2 cups Horseradish Sauce

Poach eggs and make sauce, keeping both warm while assembling dish. Arrange fish fillets on plate and gently top each with a poached egg, spooning sauce over the egg. Season to taste. (If using shrimp, place poached egg on a piece of toast or English muffin half. Add shrimp to sauce and pour over egg. Omit horseradish if desired and make a simple white sauce.) Sprinkle chives over sauce and garnish with a lemon slice.

MANGO AND NECTARINE COMPOTE
(with Berry Coulis)

In any warm climate, fruit makes for pleasurable dining. Here, the colors, as well as the flavors, combine to make the meal memorable. Two cups of any sliced or chopped fruit may be substituted.

Y I E L D : 2 cups, 4 servings

2 mangoes
2 ripe nectarines or
    peaches, or both

Peel and slice the mangoes, saving pit. Slice the nectarines and combine with mangoes in serving bowl. Holding the mango pit in one hand, squeeze to release as much juice as possible and drizzle over sliced fruit. With a perfectly ripe mango, the pit should render enough juice to create a sauce that enhances compote's flavor. Serve with Berry Coulis.

BERRY COULIS

Y I E L D : 2 cups

1 cup blueberries
1 cup raspberries
2 tablespoons sugar

Chop berries separately in food processor, adding one tablespoon sugar to each fruit. Pour separately over Mango and Nectarine Compote.

NATCHEZ-UNDER-THE-HILL ORANGE PECAN WAFFLES

❧❧❧❧❧❧❧❧❧❧❧❧❧❧❧❧❧

The pier area at Natchez is known as "Natchez-Under-the-Hill," once notorious for gambling, drinking, and dancing. Mark Twain commented rather pithily it was a place with a "desperate reputation, morally!" There were, and still are, some good places to eat in that part of town (now the area is very respectable, even chic), and pecan waffles still please tourists and natives alike.

Y I E L D : 4 servings

1/2 cup lightly toasted pecan pieces (heat in 325°F. oven for about 10 minutes; toasting enhances flavor)

1 1/3 cups all-purpose flour

2 tablespoons sugar

4 teaspoons baking powder

1/2 teaspoon salt

2 teaspoons grated orange peel (or more)

2 extra-large eggs

1/4 cup (1/2 stick) unsalted butter, melted and cooled

1 1/2 cups club soda

Combine pecan pieces, flour, sugar, baking powder, and salt in blender or food processor and whir until mixed and pecans are finely ground. Working in a large bowl, mix orange peel into dry ingredients. In another bowl, beat together eggs and butter. Add to above mixture. Add club soda, mixing thoroughly. Cook immediately on preheated waffle iron. Serve hot with melted butter and warmed cane syrup.

Note: For a tad more flavorful syrup, heat a cup of cane (or maple) syrup with 1/2 cup orange juice and serve warm. Ribbon Cane Syrup is made in Louisiana from sugar cane of the Ribbon variety. Although maple syrup has its followers, cane syrup can win many devotees through a simple taste test.

ELLIE'S BANANA FRITTERS
(with Blueberry Syrup)

Something sweet goes well in the fresh air of early morning. Fritters are a favorite, especially served with a small slice of bacon or country ham and fresh fruit.

Y I E L D : Approximately 1½ dozen fritters

½ cup milk (or 2% or skim)

2 bananas, ripe and mashed

2 cups all-purpose flour

1½ teaspoons salt

3 teaspoons baking powder

2 eggs,
 well beaten

1 tablespoon butter,
 melted

Vegetable oil for frying

Mix milk and bananas. Sift dry ingredients together. Add to fruit mixture. Add eggs and butter. Mix well. Drop by spoonfuls into 2 inches of hot oil. Turn when first side is brown. When done (about 2 minutes on each side), remove from oil and drain on paper towels. Serve hot.

Note: The above recipe, without the bananas, is a basic fritter recipe. Other fruit (approximately 2 cups) can be used—grated apples, chopped peaches or fresh berries. Also, a variation on homemade syrup can be achieved with a mixture of 1½ cups apricot preserves and ½ cup orange juice. Heat together in a sauce pan, stirring until well mixed. Serve while warm.

BLUEBERRY SYRUP

1 cup blueberries, fresh
 or frozen

¾ cup sugar

½ cup water

Cook blueberries with sugar and water until thick. Other berries can be used to make this syrup.

TUNICA INDIAN CORN PANCAKES

Keeping pancakes hot until everyone is served is not easy. Melting the butter and serving it hot, to pour over the pancakes, helps.

Health Tip: To reduce or eliminate use of oil for cooking, use no-fat butter-flavored spray on skillet and cook pancakes on hot surface.

Native American tribes lived along the banks of the lower Mississippi River and taught settlers much about farming the new land. Their resourcefulness with indigenous crops enriched the lives of countless Southerners. An ancient Indian mound called "Poverty Point" near Lake Providence, Louisiana, attests to the use by Native Americans of corn, pecans, and berries, all crops that we now take for granted. Archaeologically, this spot, now under the auspices of the U.S. government and open to visitors, is among the most important historic sites in the country. When the Cotton Blossom *travels up and down the Mississippi, the crew and cast welcome descendants of those early Indian residents, exchanging stories, songs—and recipes.*

Y I E L D : Approximately 18 pancakes, 3 inches in diameter

1 egg	1¹/2 cups *self-rising* cornmeal
1¹/4 cups milk (or 2% or skim)	(no substitute)
¹/3 cup oil	4 tablespoons oil for frying

Combine egg, milk, and oil in a bowl, and mix by hand. Add meal and mix quickly. Heat oil in a heavy skillet. Drop large spoonfuls of batter into hot oil and fry. Serve hot with butter and warm syrup.

Note: Corn pancakes go well with brunch or luncheon. Serve as a "bed" for shrimp or chicken in a cream sauce.

QUEENIE'S FLAPJACKS (without Popcorn!)

In the 1st Act, Queenie, when commenting on Joe's approach to cooking, says he would put popcorn in flapjacks if he thought it would make them turn over by themselves. Here, we honor the scene in which the cast and Julie sing "Can't Help Lovin' Dat Man of Mine."

Y I E L D : 4 servings

4 eggs, separated
1 cup sour cream (can be non-fat)
1 cup cottage cheese, small curd (can be low/non-fat)

1 cup sifted all-purpose flour
1 teaspoon baking soda
2 tablespoons sugar
2 tablespoons vegetable oil, for frying

Beat egg whites until stiff. In another bowl beat egg yolks slightly, adding other ingredients. Mix well. Fold in egg whites gently. Heat griddle or skillet to which 2 tablespoons of vegetable oil have been added. When hot, ladle ¼ cup of batter for each pancake onto surface, turning when first side is brown. Serve hot with syrup or puréed berries.

Note: Any special morning meal would include one or more meats. A fine sugar-cured bacon, thickly sliced and fried to perfection, would head the list. Of course, Southerners are fond of pork sausage (patties or links) and home-baked ham. A tray with all three favorites would thrill a river traveler—or almost anyone else.

Queenie's Tip

Sing while cooking; it makes food taste better.

Health Tip: To reduce or eliminate use of oil for cooking, use no-fat butter-flavored spray on skillet and cook pancakes on hot surface.

PAIN PERDU ("lost bread")

No presentation of Southern breakfast dishes would be complete without French toast or, as it is called in South Louisiana, pain perdu. *This recipe was created to use leftover stale French bread. If unavailable, any stale white bread can be used.*

YIELD: 4 to 6 servings

6 eggs
2 tablespoons milk
1/3 cup sugar
Grated lemon or orange rind from 1 piece of fruit
1 tablespoon orange juice or orange-flavored liqueur
8 to 12 slices stale French bread, 3/4-inch thick

Combine eggs, milk, sugar, grated rind, and juice or liqueur. Whisk until well mixed and frothy. Heat oil in skillet. Soak each slice of bread in batter for about 5 minutes. Sauté until golden brown on both sides, about 5 minutes. Drain on paper towels and serve hot with a sprinkling of confectioners' sugar, butter, and syrup.

Note: Strawberries characteristically garnish *pain perdu.* In May, the new crop suggests fancy Sunday breakfasts. Of course, other fresh fruit can be used when in season. During the winter, ribbon cane syrup most often appears with this dish.

❧ Queenie's Tip

After peeling an orange, grind rind (that has been cleaned of white pith) in the food processor and freeze in a plastic bag for future use in sauces, drinks, rice and batters. The same procedure is effective with lemon rind.

MAGNOLIA'S SWEET POTATO MUFFINS

Whether used as a vegetable or in breads and desserts, sweet potatoes occupy an important place in Southern food. Another useful food brought by the Africans, sweet potatoes have worked their way into our cuisine, thanks to good taste, versatility, and nutritive value.

YIELD: Two dozen muffins

3^1/$_2$ cups all-purpose flour
2 teaspoons baking powder
1 teaspoon soda
^{1}/$_2$ teaspoon salt
2^1/$_2$ cups sugar
^{1}/$_2$ cup cooking oil
^{1}/$_4$ cup (^{1}/$_2$ stick) butter
4 eggs
1 teaspoon allspice

1 teaspoon cinnamon
1 teaspoon nutmeg
^{2}/$_3$ cup orange juice or milk
2 teaspoons vanilla
3 cups sweet potatoes, peeled, cooked and mashed
1 cup chopped pecans

Sift all dry ingredients except sugar and spices and set aside. In a separate bowl, cream together sugar, cooking oil, butter, eggs, and spices. Gradually add dry ingredients to creamed mixture. Add orange juice (or milk) and vanilla. Fold in sweet potatoes and pecans. Pour into greased muffin tins. Bake at 325°F. for 25 to 30 minutes. Serve hot. For special occasions, serve with Creole Cream Cheese.

CREOLE CREAM CHEESE

True Creole cream cheese comes directly from New Orleans; this recipe creates a respectable substitute. It makes a delightful topping where sweetened whipped cream would be cloying on muffins or hot bread.

YIELD: 1^1/$_2$ cups

12 ounces cream cheese, softened (can be low-fat)
^{1}/$_2$ cup sour cream (can be fat-free)
1 tablespoon sugar

Combine the three ingredients and refrigerate before using.

BUTTERMILK PECAN BISCUITS

Biscuits are almost sacrosanct on the Mississippi. Whether made with buttermilk or "sweet" milk, they must be light and crisp, but not too flaky; sturdy and filling, but not too heavy. Every cook has her own secret for making the perfect biscuit.

YIELD: 2 dozen biscuits

2 cups sifted all-purpose
   flour
³/4 teaspoon salt
2 teaspoons baking powder
¹/2 teaspoon baking soda
3 heaping tablespoons solid
   vegetable shortening

1 cup buttermilk
¹/2 cup chopped pecans
   (optional)
1 tablespoon grated orange
   rind (optional)

Sift dry ingredients and cut in shortening. Pour in buttermilk and mix with fork. Add pecans and orange rind just before mixing is completed. Gather dough into firm ball and place on a floured surface. Knead for 8 "turns" and roll out dough to a ¹/2-inch thickness. Cut into desired shapes and bake on ungreased cookie sheet for 10 minutes at 450°F. These biscuits are fabulous piping hot with Fresh Strawberry Butter.

Note: We've added a twist to the standard baking powder biscuit recipe. The orange zest and pecans make a "company's coming" hot bread. If preferred, omit those two ingredients and make plain, good biscuits.

FRESH STRAWBERRY BUTTER

Some of the country's best strawberries come from Hammond and Ponchatoula, Louisiana.

YIELD: 1 cup

³/4 cup (1¹/2 sticks) butter,
   softened
³/4 cup fresh ripe
   strawberries
2 tablespoons confectioners'
   sugar

Whir all ingredients in a blender or food processor. Spread on hot biscuits or pancakes.

Note: The above can be made with other berries. Another variation: Mix grated orange rind and 2 teaspoons orange juice concentrate.

RIGHT, Natchez-Under-the-Hill with a large "O" Line boat at the dock, late 1870s.

Chapter Four

**PICNICS WHILE
CRUISIN' ON THE RIVER**

Chapter Four

Whether on land or water, picnics bring pleasure to just about everyone. Here, we remember the company and crew of the Cotton Blossom *who cruise downriver to Fort Adams, the site of their next performance. On the way, Parthy always plans an "al fresco" meal to be served in the shade of nearby trees when they reach their destination.*

JOE'S MARINATED RIVER SHRIMP

Some devotees feel that the small river shrimp have the sweetest flavor, while others demand the jumbo saltwater variety. If river shrimp are available, give them a try.

Y I E L D : 8 servings

4 pounds shrimp, boiled, shelled, and deveined
4 onions (two white, two purple), sliced
4 lemons, thinly sliced
1 tablespoon whole peppercorns
4 tablespoons capers
1 tablespoon mustard seeds
Juice of 1 lemon

$1^1/_2$ cups vegetable oil
$3/_4$ cup red or white wine vinegar
$1/_4$ cup sugar
1 teaspoon paprika
1 teaspoon cayenne pepper
2 teaspoons salt
1 teaspoon Tabasco sauce
2 cloves garlic, minced

In a large container with a lid, arrange shrimp, onion, and lemon slices in layers. Sprinkle peppercorns, capers, and mustard seeds over each layer. Mix remaining ingredients and pour over all layers. Refrigerate overnight. Serve with French bread rounds.

ELLIE'S HERBED COTTAGE CHEESE

When fresh herbs are available, they make cottage cheese a popular side dish for a summer meal; it pairs well with corn relish.

YIELD: 2 cups, 6 to 8 servings

1 pint large-curd cottage cheese

10 leaves fresh basil, washed and cut into shreds

3 sprigs fresh parsley, minced

Salt, pepper, and seasoned salt, to taste

Dash cayenne pepper, if desired

Combine all ingredients and blend gently. Serve as accompaniment with sliced tomatoes.

GOAT CHEESE IN HERBED OLIVE OIL

Another treat to take along on a picnic, this preparation goes well with the French bread rounds already being served with Joe's marinated shrimp.

YIELD: 4 to 6 servings

1 small bay leaf

4 garlic cloves, minced

1 tablespoon fresh rosemary leaves or $1/2$ teaspoon dried

Few sprigs fresh fennel or $1/4$ teaspoon seeds, crushed

$1/4$ teaspoon coriander seeds, crushed

Pinch fresh thyme or $1/2$ teaspoon dried

1 tablespoon whole peppercorns

$1/4$ to $1/2$ cup extra-virgin olive oil

1 8-ounce log mild goat cheese, cut into 8 pieces

Simmer spices and herbs in oil for 5 to 7 minutes. Place rounds of goat cheese in container with cover and pour marinade over them. Seal and refrigerate for one week for maximum taste. Can be used immediately if necessary.

Note: Packaged in a decorative jar, the Goat Cheese in Herbed Olive Oil makes a welcomed gift.

SOUTHERN FRIED CHICKEN BREAST TENDERS (with Lemon-Herb Mayonnaise)

Two food items that are dear to Southern hearts are fried chicken and homemade mayonnaise. Here the two are paired to great advantage.

Y I E L D : 4 servings

1 cup all-purpose flour
2 teaspoons salt
1 teaspoon black pepper
1 teaspoon cayenne pepper
1/2 teaspoon garlic powder
   (optional)

1 cup milk (whole or 2%)
4 large boneless, skinless
   chicken breasts, cut into
   small "fingers," about 10
   pieces per breast

Season flour with spices and place in small, flat pan. Pour milk into another small, flat pan. Dip each finger into seasoned flour, then into milk and back into flour. Fry in 2 inches of hot oil (canola is best) in a heavy skillet until thoroughly browned. Drain on paper towels and serve hot or at room temperature with Lemon-Herb *(at right)* or Cayenne Mayonnaise *(see page 79)*.

LEMON-HERB MAYONNAISE

Y I E L D : 1 1/3 cup

1 egg
2 tablespoons lemon juice
Salt and pepper to taste
1 teaspoon Dijon mustard
Fresh herbs of choice: basil,
   tarragon, dill, or parsley
1 cup light olive oil

Place egg and lemon juice in bowl of blender or food processor. Add seasonings and herbs. With feed chute of machine open and motor going, slowly pour oil into bowl. Chill and serve.

CREOLE MAYONNAISE

This is "bravo" mayonnaise!

Y I E L D : 1¹/₄ cups

1 cup mayonnaise

¹/₄ cup Creole mustard or
    other spicy mustard

¹/₃ teaspoon lemon juice

Combine all ingredients and serve
with brisket.

CHEF LOVE'S BEEF BRISKET (with Creole Mayonnaise)

Brisket is a convenient way to please stevedores and captains: it's good hot or cold, keeps well, and goes with coarse bread as well as fine biscuits.

Y I E L D : 10 to 12 servings

6 to 8 pound beef brisket with fat trimmed

3 tablespoons Worcestershire sauce

2 tablespoons black pepper

3 medium onions, sliced

6 ounces garlic, minced

Wash brisket and pat dry. Rub seasonings into meat, and place onions and garlic around brisket. Place in a greased serving dish large enough to hold the brisket. Cover tightly with foil and bake in 325°F. oven for 4 hours, or until tender. To carve meat, slice across the grain at an angle. Serve with Creole Mayonnaise.

Note: Juanita Love is the executive chef at Monmouth Plantation in Natchez. She served this dish at the opening night celebration in New York City.

PARTHENIA'S ELEGANT CHICKEN SALAD FINGER SANDWICHES

Truly good chicken salad must be made only from breast meat. The next requirement is for all ingredients to be finely chopped, even minced. Today's food processor makes this much easier.

YIELD: 2 cups, makes 2 dozen small finger sandwiches

1 1/2 cups poached chicken
   breast, chopped in
   blender or food processor
3/4 cup mayonnaise
1 tablespoon lemon juice

1/2 cup celery
1/2 cup toasted pecans,
   broken or chopped
Salt and pepper to taste

Combine all ingredients in food processor and correct seasonings. Add more mayonnaise if necessary. For making finger sandwiches, use thin-sliced white and whole wheat bread. Trim crusts and spread breads lightly with mayonnaise, then with the spreads, and cover each slice with another. Slice some sandwiches vertically, making three small sandwiches; slice others diagonally, making two larger sandwiches. Cover with plastic wrap, then with moist tea towel, and refrigerate until serving.

Note: Chill sandwich varieties separately so flavors don't "bleed" onto one another.

SPICY HAM SPREAD TEA SANDWICHES

Anytime there is leftover ham, Parthy quickly turns it into a spread for tea sandwiches or lunchtime "pick-me-ups!"

YIELD: 2 cups, makes
   2 dozen small finger
   sandwiches

1 1/2 cups baked or country
   ham, chopped in blender
   or food processor
3/4 cup mayonnaise
1 tablespoon lemon juice
3 tablespoon celery, finely
   diced
1/3 cup toasted pecans,
   broken or chopped
Pepper to taste
1 teaspoon Creole or
   "rough" mustard

Combine all ingredients and mix with a spoon, correcting seasonings. Use for sandwiches of preferred shapes.

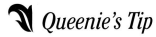

JOE'S FAVORITE BLACK-EYED PEAS AND RICE SALAD

No presentation of river food is complete without a mention of black-eyed peas and mustard greens. Joe's salad combines the two with that other basic component of Southern food: rice.

Y I E L D : 6 servings

2 cups rice, cooked

1½ cups black-eyed peas, cooked

1 10-ounce package frozen mustard greens, cooked and drained

3 green onions, sliced

¼ cup purple onion, diced

2 tomatoes, cut into chunks

¼ cup vinegar

½ cup olive oil

1 teaspoon Dijon mustard

Salt and freshly ground pepper to taste

½ teaspoon sugar

Combine first 6 ingredients. Whisk together next 6 ingredients to make vinaigrette and pour over salad. Mix well. Serve as side dish or as entrée with cooked shrimp added. High on nutrition and low on fat!

SUGAR SNAP PEA CRUDITÉ

In the early spring, when green peas are ready to be picked, gather them from the vine and pick some tendrils (if you are lucky enough to have a garden) to add for garnish and flavor. If the peas are small enough, eat raw or blanched, dipping into dressing. If larger, shell for eating.

Y I E L D : 6 servings per pound

1 pound sugar snap peas, raw and in pod

Wash peas and leave in pod. Remove strings where necessary and blanch in boiling, salted water for 1 minute. Drain, cool, and serve with Lemon-Herb Mayonnaise *(see page 55).*

Note: For a colorful winter version of a crudité, use thinly-sliced sweet potatoes. To slice, cut raw, peeled sweet potato in half lengthwise; lay flat side down on cutting board and cut thin slices from one end to the other. Turnips added to platter make colorful contrast. Cut peeled turnips in same manner.

BIBB LETTUCE SALAD

The soft green of Bibb lettuce always pleases. Here it is teamed with hearts of palm. Serve with ripe cherry tomatoes and Lemon-Herb Mayonnaise (see page 55) mixed with Balsamic Vinaigrette (see page 121).

Y I E L D : 4 to 6 servings

4 heads Bibb lettuce
6 spears hearts of palm
10 cherry tomatoes,
    cut into halves

Wash lettuce and separate leaves. Slice spears of hearts of palm into dime-sized rounds. Wash tomatoes, and toss all ingredients together.

OKRA AND TOMATOES

While stewed okra is usually served hot, like ratatouille, it can go to a picnic and add to the festivity. Bargemen, businessmen, and belles expect it to be there, hot or cold.

Y I E L D : 6 servings

1 large onion, finely chopped
1 clove garlic, minced
2 tablespoons butter (or olive oil)
8 ripe tomatoes, peeled and chopped (or one 28-ounce can), with juice
Salt and pepper to taste
2 pounds fresh okra

Sauté onion and garlic in butter or oil, and add tomatoes and seasonings. Cook covered for 15 minutes. Cut 1/2 inch off stem end of each okra pod and slice crosswise into thick "dimes." (Some cooks leave pods whole, but flavor permeates the smaller pieces.) Add okra and cook covered over reduced heat for 20 minutes or until tender. Serve hot or cold as side dish.

Note: Okra and tomatoes can be used in many incarnations: fresh corn is good mixed in. Zucchini and yellow squash, after being sautéed in oil with onions go well, as does a ground meat combination. Add eggplant and ricotta cheese, and you're almost to moussaka. It is also good topped with freshly grated Parmesan cheese. The "okra moussaka" makes a terrific entrée at a picnic or supper with a salad and hot bread.

MARINATED BROCCOLI

Another portable picnic dish that can be made ahead is fresh broccoli in a marinade. Fresh dill adds flavor.

YIELD: 8 servings

$^3/_4$ cup red wine vinegar

1 tablespoon sugar

Handful fresh dill sprigs
(or 1 tablespoon dried)

1 teaspoon salt

1 teaspoon black pepper, coarse grind

2 cloves garlic, minced

1 cup oil ($^1/_2$ vegetable oil, $^1/_2$ light
olive oil)

2 pounds fresh broccoli, cut into florets

Mix ingredients for marinade and pour over broccoli (may be raw or blanched for 2 minutes). Refrigerate for 24 hours.

Note: Fresh raw broccoli florets are good at picnics Serve with Spinach Dressing *(see page 84)* or Lemon-Herb Mayonnaise *(see page 55)* with a few shakes of curry powder added. Cauliflower and slices of red or yellow bell pepper also go well with the marinade and add extra crunch and color.

BAKES (fried biscuits) or "Floats"

The Caribbean island of Trinidad adds to the culture of the South with its cuisine, architecture, and use of available native products. Much like beignets, bakes are best when hot. Like hushpuppies, they can be made outdoors at a fish-fry for maximum enjoyment.

Y I E L D : Nine 3-inch biscuits

2 cups all-purpose flour
$1^1/2$ teaspoons baking powder
1 teaspoon salt
2 tablespoons butter, softened
$1^1/2$ teaspoons sugar dissolved in 3 tablespoons water

Sift dry ingredients into a bowl and add butter. Rub together until mixture is crumbly. Pour the sugar-water mixture into bowl and mix to make a dough. Form into 9 small balls and press flat, making rounds about 3 inches in diameter. Fry biscuits, turning to brown both sides, about 3 minutes. Drain on paper towels.

ST. FRANCISVILLE BLACKBERRY COBBLER (pictured on page 52)

❦❧❦❧❦❧❦❧❦❧❦❧❦❧❦

Upriver a few miles from Baton Rouge, St. Francisville sits on the bank of the Mississippi River. Known as the home of the world-famous Rosedown Plantation, it is also locally known for its blackberries. They are full and juicy and are difficult to save from the birds in the area; the birds know a good thing when they see it. John James Audubon painted many of the area's birds when he taught and lived at nearby Oakley Plantation. The paddlewheelers still dock at St. Francisville; some tourists stop to gather blackberries in season, before seeing the other sights.

YIELD: 8 to 10 servings

1 quart blackberries, sorted and washed
3/4 cup sugar
1/2 cup (1 stick) butter
1 cup sugar (in addition to sugar above)
1/2 cup milk (whole or 2%)
1 cup sifted all-purpose flour
1 1/2 teaspoons baking powder
Pinch salt

Mix berries with sugar. Let stand for 30 minutes or until juice forms. Melt butter in 2-quart baking dish. Make batter of remaining ingredients. Pour batter over butter. Add fruit and juice. Do not stir. Bake at 350°F. for 30 to 45 minutes or until brown. Serve warm with whipped cream, crème fraîche, or Creole Cream Cheese *(see page 49)*.

Note: Fresh peaches may also be substituted for blackberries in this recipe. Another version uses a combination of blackberries, blueberries and peaches. The colors are as pleasing as the taste!

ROSEDOWN PLANTATION HOUSE-WARMING PARTY POUND CAKE

In 1831, Martha and Daniel Turnbull completed their mansion near the Mississippi River in St. Francisville. Naming the plantation "Rosedown," after a romantic play they had seen while on their wedding trip in Europe, they brought back many ideas from the Continent for entertaining, gardening, and farming. Our Show Boat *story takes place fifty years after the Turnbulls' party. Paddlewheelers still stop to let tourists off the boat to visit Rosedown, and the pound cake is still popular up and down the river. Perfect for a party, this cake also packs well for a picnic.*

Y I E L D : 1 cake

1 cup (2 sticks) butter	1 tablespoon vanilla
1/2 cup (1 stick) margarine	Dash salt
8 ounces cream cheese	6 eggs
3 cups sugar	3 cups cake flour

Beat together butter, margarine, and cream cheese. Add sugar and cream well. Add vanilla and salt, mixing well. Add eggs, one at a time, beating well after each addition. Slowly add flour. Pour batter into 10-inch tube or bundt pan. Put pan into a *cold* oven and set dial for 275°F. Bake for 1½ hours and remove from oven. Let cake cool in pan. Serve with fresh fruit or Ambrosia *(see page 66)*. Can be made in smaller pans if several small gifts are required.

MRS. TURNBULL'S DIARY ENTRY

At their house-warming party, the Turnbulls entertained 30 guests, feeding them grandly. In her diary, Mrs. Turnbull recounted the efforts she and her staff made to ensure a satisfactory supply of food. Doubtless the guests had a good time.

"We had 30 people at our first party & we had 6 chickens for Chicken Salad, 2 Turkeys, 2 Ducks, 1 Ham, 1 Tongue, Roast Mutton, 2 Roast Chickens, 1 Pig. Henrietta took 12 dozen eggs and made a great deal of cake. It took 6 eggs for Salad, 16 pints for the Cream, Jelly, Blancmange, 50 spoon fulls of Coffe given out and not the 3rd used, 4 Decanters Wine, 4 Decanters Brandy, 8 Bottles Champaign. We had 6 lbs. Secrets and but little used, 4 lbs. candy fruit, 2 ornamental pound cakes, 12 lbs. each, 1 fruit cake, 10 lbs., 6 lbs. mixed cakes, Macaronas lady fingers and 1 Jar Grapes, 24 Bananas, 2 Hogshead Ice, 6 Pine Apples, it appears useless to make so much cake. 2 Neuga Ornaments costs 74 dollars. Musicians 60 dollars indeed to induce everything it cost 224$."

AMBROSIA

A cut-glass dish begs to be used to serve ambrosia, the most Southern of all holiday essentials. Some people believe that cut-glass bowls were invented to serve ambrosia on holiday dessert tables—or perhaps the reverse is true. Based on sectioned oranges, ambrosia also uses fresh coconut (or frozen; but please, no canned).

Y I E L D : 10 to 12 servings

5 to 6 oranges, sliced to eliminate membrane between sections

1 18½-ounce can crushed pineapple

¾ cups pecans, chopped

1 cup fresh or frozen coconut

1 6-ounce jar maraschino cherries, drained and halved

1 teaspoon confectioners' sugar (optional)

1 kiwi fruit, peeled and sliced (not traditional, but colorful)

Combine all ingredients and mix gently with hands. Serve chilled. Traditionally served with pound cake *(see page 64)* or coconut cake.

Note: Ambrosia must be freshly made to deserve a place of honor on a sideboard. During holiday festivities, cooks make it daily, in small amounts to avoid leftovers.

RIGHT, The *Lula Prince* with the "stage" lowered for unloading of people and cargo.

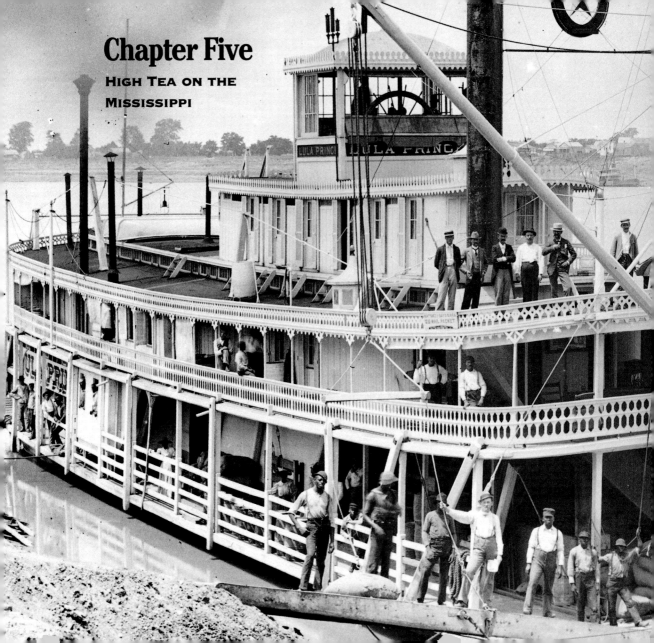

Chapter Five

High Tea on the Mississippi

Chapter Five

HIGH TEA ON THE MISSISSIPPI

Almost any situation can serve as a good reason to gather with friends. Some- times one needs no greater motivation than the fact that it's just too hot and humid and work can wait until tomorrow. Or maybe it's just too disagreeably cold. But when teatime rolls around, everything is OK.

ASSORTED FINGER SANDWICHES

The list of fillings for tea sandwiches is long, and the old rules still apply: the bread should be neatly de-crusted, and the sandwiches should be small and on the bland side. After preparing, sandwiches should be chilled. Before refrigerating, cover first with clear plastic wrap, and then a moist tea towel.

Y I E L D : To serve 8 guests, make about 4 dozen sandwiches, more if there are not many other items on the menu

- Salad of minced shrimp, homemade mayonnaise, finely diced celery, and cayenne pepper;
- Very thin tomato or cucumber slices that have been lightly salted to extract water, drained and placed on lightly buttered white bread, cut into rounds or squares;
- Sprigs of watercress on buttered white bread, chilled and rolled to form a cylinder;
- One spear of blanched asparagus on white, buttered bread rolled into a cylinder;
- Thin slices of brie with very thin tomato slices on lightly buttered white bread;
- Mixture of mayonnaise beaten with small amount of cream and a mashed pimento added to l cup of grated sharp Cheddar cheese and seasoned with salt and pepper or curry to taste;
- Mixture of mango chutney, cream cheese, minced nuts, chopped dates, cinnamon, and curry powder to taste.

SUGGESTIONS FOR A MEMORABLE TEA

❧ A large afternoon tea can be labor intensive, yet most people thoroughly enjoy this form of entertainment. If time is short, make cookies in advance and store in tins. Some sandwiches *(see recipe at right)* can be frozen.

❧ Buy a portion of the menu ready-made or prepare it with a friend. Host an afternoon tea instead of a luncheon, and see how much fun guests have.

❧ Now that tea service is making a comeback, many hotels and some restaurants offer tea in the afternoons. Visit a few of these establishments to pick up ideas.

❧ In hot weather, use iced tea or the recipe for Frosted Minted Lemonade *(see page 90)* or make a punch of fresh orange, mango, apricot nectar, and lemon juice. Add a splash of seltzer if desired.

TEA SANDWICHES FOR THE FREEZER

Having a few "goodies" in the freezer is like having money in the bank: it always comes in handy. These sandwiches can be thawed and ready to serve in about 1 hour.

YIELD: Filling for approximately 1½ dozen small sandwiches

8 ounces cream cheese, softened (can be low-fat)

¾ chopped walnuts or pecans

¼ green bell pepper, chopped

¼ cup onion, chopped

1 tablespoon canned pimento, mashed

3 eggs, hard boiled, in small dice

Salt and pepper to taste

Combine all ingredients and spread on bread. Cut into desired shapes and freeze until needed. At serving time, garnish with fresh parsley.

Note: Chill first in a single layer on a cookie sheet; then pack in plastic bags to freeze.

U.S.S. CAIRO COFFEE AND PECAN SPONGE CAKE (with Frosting)

Named after the ironclad vessel that sank at Vicksburg during the Civil War, this light cake is good enough to be a peacemaker. Despite the use of pecans, the recipe is of English origin and pays respect to the affinity between England and the American South.

Y I E L D : 8-inch cake, 2 layers

1 cup (2 sticks) butter
1 cup dark brown sugar
4 extra-large eggs
1 2/3 cups *self-rising* flour, sifted
3 tablespoons strong black coffee
1 cup pecans, broken
1 teaspoon vanilla

Cream together butter and sugar until light. Add the eggs one by one to sugar mixture, beating after each addition. Add flour, coffee, nuts, and vanilla, and beat gently to mix. Pour batter into two greased 8-inch cake pans and bake in a 350°F. oven for 20 to 25 minutes. When completely cool, ice with coffee Buttercream Frosting.

COFFEE BUTTERCREAM FROSTING

Y I E L D : Enough icing for a 2-layer cake, top and sides

1/2 cup (1 stick) unsweetened butter, softened
2 cups confectioners' sugar
1/4 cup cream, table or whipping
6 tablespoons strong black coffee
1 teaspoon vanilla
Pecan halves for decoration

Cream together butter and sugar, and add cream, coffee, and vanilla. Beat until well mixed. Frost cooled cake. Decorate with pecan halves.

Note: If desired, cake can "go to tea" decorated with edible flowers, such as pansies.

BATTURE BUTTER-OATMEAL COOKIES

On the Mississippi River, visible from the water, a band of trees stretches from the water's edge up toward the levee. The French settlers called this area the "batture." Technically, it is made up of the land formed by the bed of a river. During various periods of history, this piece of land has been the subject of ownership disputes: is it public property, or does the adjacent landowner claim it as his own? What about the mineral rights? Those questions are difficult ones, but this cookie recipe is easy.

YIELD: Approximately 4 dozen

1 cup (2 sticks) butter
1/2 cup white sugar
1/2 cup dark brown sugar
2 egg yolks

2 teaspoons vanilla
1 1/4 cups all-purpose flour
1 1/2 cups quick oats

Cream butter and white sugar. Add brown sugar and continue beating. Add egg yolks and vanilla, and blend well. Add flour and mix; add oats and mix well. Drop mixture in small teaspoons onto cookie sheet and bake at 375°F. for 8 to 10 minutes. Store in tins when cool. Store uncooked dough in refrigerator or freeze it.

MORE SUGGESTIONS FOR A MEMORABLE TEA

❧ To make a good cup of tea, fill teapot with boiling water, then boil more water to make the tea. Leave teapot to get really hot, then pour out water. Bring teapot to the boiling water; fill and let heat for 2 minutes with top on pot.

❧ Offer milk (not cream), lemon slices, and sugar.

❧ Keep water in kettle simmering in kitchen to dilute tea after initial cup has been served.

CAT'S TONGUES COOKIES
(Langues-de-Chat)

Teatime requires a certain delicacy in the food served— it should be rich but also a little bland. A deep chocolate brownie, although tasty, would overpower the flavor of the tea. Cat's Tongues are crisp, buttery, and lightly sweet. They go well with fruit or ice cream.

Y I E L D : About 2$\frac{1}{2}$ dozen cookies

$\frac{1}{4}$ cup ($\frac{1}{2}$ stick) unsalted butter, softened	Whites of 2 extra-large eggs
$\frac{1}{3}$ cup sugar	$\frac{1}{3}$ cup all-purpose flour
Rind of l lemon, grated	Splash of vanilla (less than $\frac{1}{4}$ teaspoon)

Cream butter, sugar, and lemon rind with mixer until light and fluffy. Do not overbeat to limpness. Gradually stir in egg whites, about $\frac{1}{2}$ tablespoon at a time, with a wooden spoon just long enough to integrate egg white but don't beat. Add the vanilla. Sift $\frac{1}{4}$ of flour into dough in the bowl, working with spoon to integrate each addition. Continue until flour is used, adding $\frac{1}{4}$ of flour each time. Spoon dough into pastry tube, and pipe dough onto two large cookie sheets that have been greased and floured. Pipe dough in straight strokes about $\frac{1}{2}$ inch by 3 inches—something resembling a "cat's tongue!" Bake in 425°F. oven for 6 to 8 minutes. Take out when edges of cookies begin to brown. Remove from cookie sheet and store in airtight tin when cool.

MORE SUGGESTIONS FOR A MEMORABLE TEA

❧ A guest feels really well treated when served tea made from loose tea. Buy a tea strainer and dazzle someone as you serve tea the "fancy" way. If tea bags are being used, offer more than one variety.

❧ Garnish finger sandwiches with your favorite fresh snipped herbs.

❧ An assortment of buttery cookies—"sables"—makes for happy nibbling.

❧ Remember that tea need not suggest a large crowd; invite one friend whom you haven't seen for a while. Getting together over a few sandwiches and a cookie makes for good catch-up time.

❧ Keep a tea pot handy so calling that friend won't seem like an effort.

❧ Invite a child or two to have tea; children relish being treated like a grown-up. And, of course, they love sweets!

ROSE BUTTER

(pictured on page 1)

Of all the flowers common to the South, the rose is among the best loved. Its color adds to any centerpiece; the taste and fragrance of the petals add a heavenly dimension to butter for tea scones.

YIELD: 1/2 cup

1/2 cup (1 stick) unsalted
     butter
1 cup rose petals, cut into
     a chiffonade (shredded)
1/2 teaspoon salt

Cream butter and add remaining ingredients; mix well. If desired, roll butter into logs and freeze for later use. Serve at room temperature.

Note: Flowers are popular as edibles now; other blossoms may be substituted, but be sure they are organically grown and can be eaten safely.

DRIED FRUIT SCONES

In the British Isles, where tea service is a fact of life, scones are the bread of life. Slightly sweeter than biscuits, but less sweet than a cookie, they provide the perfect reason to indulge in Rose Butter, good preserves or clotted cream. On the Cotton Blossom Floating Palace Theatre, *Queenie's quick breads are known up and down the river; scones, like biscuits, are one of her specialties.*

YIELD: 30 small or 15 large scones

2 cups sifted all-purpose
     flour
2 tablespoons sugar
1 tablespoon baking powder
1/2 teaspoon salt
5 tablespoons butter
1 egg, beaten
3/4 cup milk
1/2 to 3/4 cup dried currants,
     cranberries, or cherries
     (optional)

Sift together dry ingredients. Cut in butter with fork or pastry blender until mixture resembles cornmeal. Add egg and almost all the milk. Stir with a fork until flour is absorbed. Add desired dried fruit. Add more milk if too dry (you should be able to roll out dough on floured surface). Knead dough for about 10 "turns" and roll to 1/2-inch thickness. Cut out with a small biscuit cutter; place on greased baking sheet. Bake in 425°F. oven for about 12 minutes. Serve scones hot or at room temperature with clotted cream, preserves or Rose Butter.

SYRUP AND GINGER BUTTERMILK SCONES (with Rum Butter)

Scones appear in countless recipes and, like bagels, take every incarnation from cheese, herb, fruit to plain. Here, the addition of cane syrup, ginger, and buttermilk creates a very different result, one that can go with jams, cream, or ham and turkey. This version surprises and delights; the use of self-rising flour makes the mixing very quick and easy.

YIELD: 24 small or 12 large scones

1 2/3 cups *self-rising* flour

1 teaspoon ground ginger

2 tablespoons brown sugar

1/4 cup (1/2 stick) butter

1 tablespoon cane syrup
  or dark Karo syrup

2/3 cup buttermilk

1 tablespoon milk,
  for glaze

Sift the flour with the ginger and add the sugar. Cut the butter into the flour and mix until dough looks like cornmeal. Heat syrup and mix with buttermilk. Make a well in the center of the mixture and add liquid. Mix quickly and pour onto floured surface; knead until smooth. Roll out to about 3/4-inch thick and cut into desired shapes. Brush with milk. Bake in 450°F. oven for 8 to 10 minutes.

RUM BUTTER

YIELD: About 3/4 cup

1 cup brown sugar

1/4 teaspoon nutmeg, freshly
  grated

2 to 3 tablespoons dark rum

1/2 cup (1 stick) unsalted
  butter, melted

Mix all ingredients except butter, then mix in melted butter. Let set before using.

The *Belle Memphis* steams up the river with the lowlands of Louisiana and one of the many bends of the lower Mississippi in the distance. The large side-wheeler carried passengers, freight and mail.

Chapter Six

HORS D'OEUVRES
ON THE UPPER DECK

Chapter Six

Early on summer evenings, the upper deck of a steamboat provides a scenic spot for drinks and hors d'oeuvres. (That's where Magnolia and Gaylord confess their love on a moonlit night, singing "You Are Love.")

ELLIE'S CRISP BLANCHED OKRA STICKS (with Cayenne Mayonnaise)

Perhaps no other vegetable is so evocative of the South as okra. Brought with the first Africans, it has improved our cuisine immeasurably. Used here as a cold hors d'oeuvre, the sticks are crunchy and pair well with the spicy mayonnaise.

YIELD: Approximately 24 okra sticks

1 1/2 pounds fresh baby okra (use only fresh, small pods)
1 teaspoon salt

Cut stem end from all okra pods. Drop okra into boiling salted water. Cook 2 to 3 minutes and remove to platter to cool. (Pods should be bright green and resistant to bite. Do not overcook, as crispness is part of the appeal.)

CAYENNE MAYONNAISE

YIELD: 1 cup

1 cup mayonnaise
2 teaspoons fresh lemon juice
1/2 teaspoon cayenne pepper (or more)
Dash hot sauce

Mix all ingredients and serve as a dip with crisp okra sticks—or Fried Chicken Tenders *(see page 55)* or cold boiled shrimp.

RIVER BOTTOM ROASTED PECANS

It is impossible to eat just one of these spicy roasted pecans! They are a good accompaniment for cheeses and water biscuits.

YIELD: 2 cups

1/4 cup (1/2 stick) butter

1 tablespoon Worchestershire sauce

1 teaspoon hot sauce (Tabasco or other)

1 teaspoon salt

1/4 teaspoon cayenne pepper

1/2 teaspoon chili powder

2 cups pecan halves

In a cast iron skillet (or other heavy pan) melt butter. Add seasonings and mix. Add pecans, stirring over low heat until nuts begin to brown. Remove from heat and spread on greased baking sheet. Roast at 200°F. for 20 to 30 minutes. Can be stored in tightly-sealed tin and kept fresh for two weeks.

CURRIED CHEESE AND CHUTNEY SPREAD

═══════════════════════════════════════

During a cocktail party, it's fun to watch guests sample this spread and come back for more, as if to say, "I can't imagine what is in this; let me try it again." Soon the dish is empty, and still no one can identify the ingredients, and everyone wants more.

Y I E L D : About 2$1/2$ cups, enough for approximately
   8 to 10 servings

8 ounces cream cheese, softened (can be low-fat)

1 cup sharp cheese, grated

$1/2$ to 1 teaspoon curry powder, more if desired

3 tablespoons sherry

1 8-ounce jar Major Grey's mango chutney

$1/2$ cup green onions, chopped

Combine cream cheese and sharp cheese, then add curry powder and sherry. Mound onto serving dish. Pour chutney over cheese and top with green onions. Serve with crackers.

Note: This spread makes a good tea sandwich. Omit onions and use wheat bread.

Use pecans in more dishes;
they are very good for you. Use
them in salads, breads, with
cheese, or eat them raw. Too often
they are used only in sweet desserts.

VICKSBURG CHEESE-PECAN COCKTAIL WAFERS

All the talk about Southern hospitality is absolutely true. Vicksburg beckons visitors. Its history, along with its hospitality, promises a good stay with fine food. Whenever visitors drop by, we feel they deserve to be offered some form of sustenance. In order not to get caught with an empty larder, we keep this sort of treat ready in tins or unbaked in the freezer, waiting to be popped into a hot oven. We're seldom more than 10 minutes away from graciousness.

YIELD: 6 to 7 dozen wafers

1 cup pecans, finely chopped
1 cup sharp Cheddar cheese, grated
1 cup all-purpose flour, sifted
1/2 cup (1 stick) butter or margarine, softened
1 teaspoon salt
1/8 teaspoon (or more) cayenne pepper

Combine all ingredients in large bowl and mix by hand. Divide dough (it will be stiff) in half and shape into two logs about the diameter of a quarter. Wrap each log in waxed paper, and chill for at least an hour. Slice logs into 1/4-inch wafers and bake at 350°F. for 10 to 12 minutes.

Note: These wafers can be frozen unbaked, or baked and stored in tins.

GAYLORD'S BLEU CHEESE-WALNUT SPREAD

❧≈❧≈❧≈❧≈❧≈❧≈❧≈❧≈❧

*Like Gaylord, this hors d'oeuvre spread is velvety and appeals
to just about everyone. Served with melba toast rounds and
other mild crackers, it goes well with drinks before dinner
or with port afterward.*

Y I E L D : 2 cups

12 ounces bleu cheese, crumbled
8 ounces cream cheese, softened (can be low-fat)
1 tablespoon dried chives
Splash of vermouth (optional)
3/4 cup walnut pieces

Combine all ingredients except the walnuts in a bowl and shape with
hands into desired shape or loaf. Spread nuts on flat surface and roll
cheese ball until covered. Serve at room temperature; chill to store.
This cheese mixture also goes particularly well with a spinach salad
(see page 121).

(see page 121).

Queenie's Tip

*To enhance the flavor of walnuts
and pecans in a recipe, toast them
for about 10 minutes in a 300°F.
oven.*

SPINACH DRESSING

This dressing goes well with any crudité, and it can be spread on a turkey or roast beef sandwich. With thin slices of smoked turkey breast, it makes a nice tea sandwich.

YIELD: 1½ cups

2 10-ounce boxes frozen, chopped spinach, thawed

½ cup green onions, chopped

1½ cups mayonnaise

Dash lemon juice

1 teaspoon nutmeg

1 teaspoon garlic powder (or more, if desired)

2 tablespoons fresh dill or 1 teaspoon dried

1 teaspoon celery seed

Squeeze water from thawed spinach until very dry. Combine all ingredients in small bowl, and let stand an hour before serving.

WHITE TURNIP CRUDITÉ
(with Spinach Dressing)

The turnip is another vegetable integral to the South. The greens give us a popular cooked dish, and often the root is used with them. Here, the bottom is used raw, giving off a peppery taste that pairs well with the spinach dressing.

YIELD: 8 servings

6 medium turnips, peeled and sliced crosswise, cut as potatoes are cut for thick chips

After slicing, drop turnips into ice water to prevent darkening. Drain and serve with Spinach Dressing. If assorted crudités are used, include a pared and sliced jicama and raw vegetables of varying colors to provide eye appeal.

Health Tip: In Spinach Dressing, reduced-fat mayonnaise can be used. To further reduce fat content, reduce the amount of mayonnaise used to 1 cup. Dressing will only be more "spinachy," therefore, healthier.

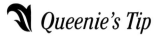

Queenie's Tip

When using salt, use sea salt; it comes in coarse and fine grind and has more vitamins and minerals. Of course, the fine grind is all-purpose; use as you would any other salt.

QUEENIE'S CAJUN POPCORN

After passing through New Orleans so many times, Queenie picked up some seasoning tips that make treats out of mundane snacks.

Y I E L D : Fills a 2 quart bowl

¹/₂ cup popcorn, unpopped
1 teaspoon salt
1 teaspoon chili powder
Dash cayenne pepper
1 teaspoon dried parsley
1 teaspoon imitation butter flavoring

Pop high-quality popcorn according to package directions. Mix spices and sprinkle over popcorn while hot.

Note: For an Italian twist, add 1 tablespoon freshly grated Parmesan cheese and toss.

RIGHT, The *Liberty*, built in 1889, had 26 staterooms and was allowed to carry a hundred passengers.

Chapter Seven

DRINKS ON THE LEVEE

Chapter Seven

The levee is an embankment on either side of the river, about 15 feet high, built to protect low areas from flooding. In the South, it has served as the setting for many literary romantic fantasies— the site of arrivals and new hope, or departures and sad farewells. Throughout the year, people enjoy strolling on the levee. However, on Christmas Eve, bonfires are built there to beckon Père Nöel (Santa Claus). When the steamboat docks, tourists race from the vessel to the top of this man-made wall, eager to see the splendid plantation houses that line the River Road. At the crest of the hill, sojourners enjoy some local refreshments.

MISSISSIPPI SIPPIN' ICED TEA

Along the river iced tea is considered survival fare; it beats the heat like nothing else. While simple iced tea suffices at meal time, a "fancied up" version is required to get through sticky afternoons.

YIELD: Approximately 1 gallon

2 cups sugar

2 cups water

1 quart hot water

8 tea bags (or 8 teaspoons loose tea in a tea ball)

2 quarts cold water (1 quart can be club soda)

2 cups orange juice

3/4 cup lemon juice (preferably freshly squeezed)

Mint sprigs for garnish

Boil sugar and 2 cups water for 5 minutes. Add 1 quart hot water and tea bags. Steep for 5 minutes. Discard tea bags (or remove tea ball). Add cold water, orange juice, and lemon juice, mixing thoroughly. Serve over crushed ice. Add mint sprigs when serving.

Note: For a more punch-like cooler, add club soda or ginger ale, along with pineapple juice. A small cluster of green grapes hung on the side of the glass goes nicely with this beverage.

LEFT, *(left to right)* Frosted Minted Lemonade; Ramos Gin Fizz; Mississippi Sippin' Iced Tea; Delta Planters' Punch; Mimosa; and Frank's Milk Punch.

MISSISSIPPI BREEZE

Use lemonade recipe to make a really cooling "spiked" summer drink. Afficionados in some areas call it a "Bayou Breeze;" others use the name "Mississippi Breeze." Whatever it is called, it is guaranteed to please.

Add the desired amount of Coconut Rum (available in expansive liquor stores) and pour ingredients into a punchbowl filled with crushed ice. Substitute pineapple juice for the crushed pineapple for easier sipping. Garnish bowl or individual glasses with mint sprigs.

FROSTED MINTED LEMONADE

A sprig of fresh rosemary provides an unexpected taste treat. Instead of using it as a garnish, add it to the drink itself.

YIELD: Approximately 2 1/2 quarts

1 cup sugar

1 pint water

1 20-ounce can crushed pineapple, with juice

Rind and juice of 4 lemons

Rind and juice of 1 lime

1 quart cold water

l to 2 sprigs fresh rosemary

Mint sprigs for garnish

Make a syrup by boiling the sugar and water for 10 minutes. Add the pineapple with juice, lemon rind and juice, and lime rind and juice. Cool, strain, and add cold water and rosemary. Serve over ice, garnished with mint.

Note: Lemonade should be poured from a pitcher and served in a tall or stemmed glass. If weather permits, drink it while sitting under a shade tree while watching the river as it "keeps on rolling along."

Variation: Puree 1/2 cup of blueberries and add to above mixture for a visual treat. Garnish with lemon slice.

STRAWBERRY "DAIQUIRI" (nonalcoholic)

Crushed ice and fresh strawberries combine to create a popular "cooler." One has fun deciding whether to eat it or drink it.

YIELD: 1 to 2 drinks

1 cup fresh, ripe strawberries
Juice of 2 limes
2 tablespoons Simple Syrup *(see recipe, page 96)*
1 cup crushed ice
Pineapple spear, whole berries or mint sprigs for garnish

Combine first four ingredients in a blender or food processor and whir for 30 to 40 seconds. Serve in tall, frosted glass with garnish.

Note: Fruit drinks can be as varied as the season. Other fruits, such as bananas, mangoes, or berries, can be substituted. Garnish with whatever is fresh, colorful and tasty. Sprigs of herbs such as rose geranium also add interest. This is a basic nonalcoholic daiquiri formula. If alcohol is preferred, add 3 ounces of white rum before blending.

Queenie's Tip

Iced drinks always "sweat" as moisture collects on the glass. Always serve drinks with napkins and/or coasters to prevent a water ring when the glass is set on a wooden surface.

DELTA PLANTERS' PUNCH

Although Greek Revival plantation houses come to mind when tourists visit the South, many homes in Louisiana were built in the French planter fashion. Copied directly from the architecture of Martinique and Haiti, those structures proved suitable for the semitropical climate where ventilation was essential. Planters' punch, another gift from the islands, also afforded some comfort.

Y I E L D : 2 strong drinks or, diluted with juice or water,
   4 weak ones

1/2 cup fresh orange juice (4 ounces)

1/2 cup pineapple juice (4 ounces)

2 ounces white rum

2 ounces dark rum

Dash grenadine syrup (available in liquor stores)

Dash Angostura bitters (also in liquor stores)

Spears of fresh pineapple for garnish

Sprigs of fresh mint for garnish

Combine juices, rums, grenadine, and bitters in a pitcher. Pour entire potion over ice cubes into tall frosted glasses. Garnish with pineapple and mint.

RAMOS GIN FIZZ

The frothiness provided by the egg white deceives the drinker, tricking him into downing a second one. Be watchful. Created in New Orleans during the height of the steamboat era, the Ramos Gin Fizz caused some unsuspecting travelers to be carried back to the boat just in time to leave port!

YIELD: 1 drink

1 egg white, beaten to a froth
1 teaspoon confectioners' sugar
Dash orange flower water (available in liquor stores)
Juice of $1/2$ lime
1 drop vanilla
2 tablespoons whipping cream
2 ounces gin ($1/4$ cup)
3 tablespoons club soda
Orange slice for garnish

Combine all ingredients in a cocktail shaker and shake vigorously until contents are thick and creamy. Serve in a tall glass over cracked ice and garnish with orange slice. (This drink really beats the heat; try it as an afternoon drink by replacing gin with 2 ounces of orange juice concentrate.)

Note: Composed drinks, *i.e.* potions that must be stirred, whirred, shaken or frothed, have been a fixture of elegant parties. Like the Mint Julep, the Ramos Gin Fizz derives part of its appeal from the ritual of preparation.

MINT SIMPLE SYRUP

Mint julep devotees keep a bottle of the mint simple syrup handy to speed preparation.

Y I E L D : About 1½ cups, enough for about 10 drinks

3 cups sugar
1 cup water
2 handsful fresh mint sprigs

Combine sugar with water in a 2-quart saucepan. Add enough mint to fill pan loosely. Boil 5 or 6 minutes, or until liquid turns green. Strain syrup and pour into bottle for future use. Chill.

MINT JULEP

A presentation of Southern food and drink must include the mint julep. It is traditionally served in a silver "cup"—more like a tumbler than a cup—designed especially for juleps. Very strong, the julep should be drunk advisedly and slowly.

Y I E L D : 1 drink

Crushed ice
3 ounces whiskey, per glass
1 ounce (2 tablespoons) chilled Mint Simple Syrup
    (recipe at left)
Maraschino cherries with stems
Confectioners' sugar for coating cherries
Mint sprigs for garnish (in addition to mint for cooking
    with the syrup)

Fill a 10-ounce serving glass (preferably a silver julep cup) with crushed ice. Add whiskey and chilled Mint Simple Syrup. Dip cherry into confectioners' sugar. Garnish julep with coated cherry and mint sprigs.

MIMOSA

Who can forget the pungent, sweet smell of the mimosa blossom? Its scent permeates the still night air of a summer evening. Re-create the colors of the flower with this lovely drink.

Y I E L D : 1 drink

3 ounces champagne
3 ounces orange juice (preferably freshly squeezed)
1 whole ripe strawberry
1 orange slice

Pour champagne into a stemmed glass. Add orange juice. Drop strawberry into the glass, garnishing rim of glass with orange slice.

Note: More pink than orange, a mimosa flower is delicate and soothing. Mimosas are a good "house drink" at a Sunday brunch, lightening the duties of a bartender and offering a gentle non-lethal drink from a pitcher or punch bowl.

Queenie's Tip

Make Cajun Mimosas by steeping pickled sliced Tabasco or jalapeño peppers in the orange juice overnight.

SIMPLE SYRUP

YIELD: 1 cup

1 cup sugar
1/2 cup water

Combine sugar and water in small saucepan and boil for 5 minutes. Store unused portion in glass jar in refrigerator.

FRANK'S MILK PUNCH Á LA TROCADERO

Magnolia might drink this punch to cheer herself up on New Year's Day morning. Milk Punch is traditionally served in the morning, when it's too early for Bloody Marys! This drink incorporates some of the smoothness of egg nog with the "iciness" of a mixed drink.

YIELD: 1 serving

1 cup ice cubes
1 1/2 ounces Napoleon brandy or bourbon
2 tablespoons Simple Syrup *(recipe at left)*
1/2 cup half-and-half (or whole or 2% milk)
1 teaspoon vanilla
Pinch nutmeg

Combine first five ingredients in a cocktail shaker. Shake vigorously, then pour into a chilled old-fashioned glass. Sprinkle with nutmeg and serve.

WATERMELON YOGURT SMOOTHIE

Perhaps no other fruit evokes images of the South more than watermelon. Its colors, taste, and texture endear it to children and adults. When whirred in the blender or the food processor, a uniquely refreshing drink results. Here, we team it with yogurt and come out with a meal in a glass.

YIELD: 1 quart

1 whole banana, frozen in peel
   (freezing adds thickness)
1 pint plain non-fat yogurt
1 cup skim milk
2 cups watermelon, diced and
   seeded
Watermelon spears for garnish

Peel banana and add to bowl of blender or food processor. Whir to mash. Add remaining ingredients and continue to whir until frothy. Serve in tall glass with fresh watermelon spears for garnish. Some enjoy a bit of club soda added after blending.

PERFECT NEW ORLEANS CAFÉ AU LAIT

Today's cappuccino craze echoes the traditional Louisiana passion for café au lait. Chicory was used during the Civil War when coffee was unavailable; being a native root, it proved an effective substitute. After the war, coffee drinkers decided to continue its use, mixing it with French roast coffee beans. Everything depends on starting with the right coffee beans—then the addition of chicory completes the mixture. If one is a purist, order the blend from Café du Monde in New Orleans, (504) 581-2914. The flavor is rich and never harsh. The company has a direct-mail service and also ships its beignet mix.

YIELD: 8 servings

5 tablespoons dark roast coffee with chicory, drip grind
4 cups boiling water
4 cups hot milk, whole or 2 percent

Prepare coffee. Heat milk separately. When coffee has brewed, pour equal portions of hot milk and coffee simultaneously into coffee cups.

SWEET CAFÉ AU LAIT

For coffee drinkers who like it sweet, the following method of caramelizing sugar and combining it with milk makes the beverage entirely authentic. This recipe is not for those who like their coffee unsweetened, however.

YIELD: 4 servings

3 tablespoons sugar
2 cups boiling milk
2 cups coffee (made according to recipe at right)

In a heavy saucepan, cook sugar over low heat, stirring until it caramelizes to a dark nutty color (about 7 minutes). Remove from heat and add milk slowly—hot sugar sputters when liquid meets it. Mix well, then stir into hot coffee. The added caramel flavor is sumptuous, but sweet.

RIGHT, The big side-wheeler James Howard at the landing, tieing up to the wharfboat.

Chapter Eight

Fancy Dress Suppers, Dinners and "After the Ball" Parties

Chapter Eight

An evening meal with friends can become an unforgettable experience with foods that bespeak a celebration. Truly delicious food is available for any occasion, whether the meal itself is an early, casual outdoor supper, a late-night formal dinner or a wee-hours-of-the-morning breakfast. Presentation also enhances the theme established by the menu. These recipes suggest a range of entertaining styles that provide the host with some latitude. He or she can stay within a tight budget or splurge to the outer limits of extravagance!!

CARRIAGE HOUSE TOMATO ASPIC

Served at the Show Boat *opening night gala in New York City, this dramatically colorful, spicy, cool aspic lends festivity to any buffet. Deliciously low in fat and calories.*

YIELD: 12 servings

1/2 cup boiling water
2 envelopes unflavored gelatin
3 cups tomato juice, warmed
1/2 teaspoon Tabasco
1 small onion, finely minced
2 ribs celery, very finely minced

1 tablespoon freshly squeezed lemon juice
2 teaspoons Worcestershire sauce
1 teaspoon salt
1/2 teaspoon black pepper, freshly ground
8 ounces cream cheese

Pour boiling water into a bowl and sprinkle gelatin over it. When gelatin is completely dissolved, stir in the warmed tomato juice until smooth. Stir in all other ingredients except cream cheese and cool slightly. Meanwhile, dot the bottom of a large ring mold with spoonfuls of cream cheese. Pour tomato mixture into mold and refrigerate until set.

Note: In the summer, a luncheon can be built around this aspic, putting luxurious lump crabmeat or boiled jumbo shrimp in the center of the ring. Traditionally, fresh green beans in a mild vinaigrette are served as the side dish, along with Boston lettuce and hot rolls.

ROASTING TABLE FOR TENDERLOIN

Rare: 35 minutes

Medium: 40 minutes

Medium well: 45 minutes

Remove meat from oven and let it rest for 15 minutes before slicing crosswise to serve.

FANCIEST-NIGHT-OF-THE-YEAR TENDERLOIN OF BEEF

On those occasions when Gaylord's "ship comes in," he likes to celebrate with a really special dinner and this is the dish he orders.

Y I E L D : 8 servings

1 whole beef tenderloin (5 to 6 pounds)

6 cloves garlic, peeled and slivered

MARINADE

1 cup soy sauce

$1/4$ cup olive oil

$1/2$ teaspoon Tabasco

1 cup port wine, cooking quality

1 teaspoon black pepper

1 teaspoon dried thyme or a fresh sprig

1 bay leaf

Ask butcher to trim and tie tenderloin. Make small slits in meat and insert garlic slivers. Place meat in large bowl. Combine all ingredients for marinade and pour over meat. Leave meat to marinate in refrigerator overnight or for at least 6 hours. Remove meat from marinade and place on roasting pan. Preheat oven to 425°F. Roast meat according to desired doneness.

CREOLE PLANTATION GRITS

Grits are coarsely ground corn kernels. More finely-ground corn yields corn meal. Grits are packaged several ways, according to the length of cooking time. "Old-fashioned" grits have a lengthy cooking time of 30 minutes during which they must be stirred frequently to avoid sticking and lumps. "Quick" grits are flavorful and can be cooked in only 5 minutes. Avoid the "instant" grits, they are never very tasty. Properly cooked, grits have a creamy, uniform texture.

Y I E L D : 8 servings

2 teaspoons salt	1/4 cup (1/2 stick) butter
4 1/2 cups water	1 teaspoon pepper
1 cup grits	

In a medium saucepan, bring salted water to boil. Gradually add grits, stirring constantly. Reduce heat and simmer until thickened to desired consistency (5 to 10 minutes). Add butter and pepper, and mix well. Serve hot as a side dish.

Note: Cooked grits like Italian polenta can be mixed with grated cheese and minced garlic and baked at 350°F. for 20 minutes to serve with grillades (beef round steak smothered in gravy with peppers and tomatoes), a favorite meal for Mardi Gras. Leftover cheese grits can be cut into squares and sautéed in 1 tablespoon olive oil.

Queenie's Tip

After cooking grits, remove to a serving dish and immediately fill the cooking pan with cold water. Any remaining grits will not stick and the pan will be wonderfully easy to clean.

ROAST PORK TENDERLOIN
(with Wild Rice-Pecan Dressing)

Perfect for a winter holiday meal, this dish brings in the New Year in a wonderful way.

Y I E L D : 8 servings

Pork tenderloins (about 3
    pounds)
4 tablespoons soy sauce

Put meat (two pieces in each package kept together, but no need to tie them) into baking dish. Pour soy sauce over meat and let it marinate about 1 hour, time permitting; it's not essential. Bake in 350°F. oven for 1 hour. Serve hot or cold, slicing into 1/2-inch thick medallions—no thicker.

Note: This dish is as versatile as any can be. It is good in summer or winter, hot or cold, freshly made or as a leftover, and it is less fattening than most meat! Pairs well with a cold curried rice salad or the following wild rice/white rice combination.

WILD RICE-PECAN DRESSING

Native American wild rice blends with pecans and white rice for interesting textures and earthy exotic flavors.

Y I E L D : 8 servings

1 cup long-grain white or converted rice

1/2 cup wild rice

Chicken broth (defatted) enough to cover rice by 1 inch

1 tablespoon butter or olive oil (optional)

1 tablespoon orange rind, grated

1/4 cup orange juice

Salt and pepper to taste

1 teaspoon fresh garlic or garlic powder

Few sprigs fresh parsley, minced

1/2 cup toasted pecans, broken

Orange slices and whole kumquats for garnish

Combine all ingredients except pecans and garnishes in saucepan and cook, covered, until water boils down to level of rice. Lower heat and continue to cook for about 30 minutes, being careful not to burn on bottom. (Heat should be very low.) Test for doneness of wild rice (white rice will be soft) and continue cooking another 15 minutes or until wild rice is soft. When serving, toss pecans with rice mixture and garnish with orange slices and whole kumquats. Serve with cranberries in some form, preferably cranberry chutney.

Queenie's Tip

Have a few friends over for a meal. Cook dishes from this cookbook, and play music from Show Boat *while eating.*

MAYOR'S WIFE'S PECAN-ENCRUSTED CHICKEN BREASTS

Each time the Cotton Blossom *returns to a location, the cast, crew, and local townspeople get together to celebrate their reunion. At Fort Adams, they frequently have a dockside twilight potluck dinner, with many people bringing their specialties. The menu stays pretty much the same from one season to the next. This recipe is the Mayor's wife's contribution. With an abundance of pecans, a cook can work wonders. In Fort Adams, this dish was basic to any potluck dinner.*

YIELD: 8 servings

8 boneless, skinless chicken breasts

Salt and pepper to taste

Dash cayenne pepper

1 cup pecan pieces, ground in food processor or finely minced

1/4 cup olive oil

1/4 cup (1/2 stick) butter

Salt and pepper each chicken breast on both sides. Mix cayenne pepper with ground pecans on flat surface covered with waxed paper and dredge each chicken breast until coated thoroughly on both sides. Add more pecans to surface if needed to make thick coating. Heat mixture of oil and butter in skillet and sauté chicken breast until brown, 5 to 8 minutes on each side (depending on size). Serve hot or cold.

FORT ADAMS FRIED OKRA

In the South, when someone professes to not like okra prepared in any fashion, he is offered fried okra. It is assumed that frying anything will make it at least tolerable if not palatable! Usually it works.

Y I E L D : 6 to 8 servings

2 pounds fresh, young okra	1 teaspoon salt
1 cup corn meal	1/2 teaspoon pepper
1/2 cup all-purpose flour	Oil for frying

Cut stem end off okra and cut each pod into "dimes" about 1/4-inch thick. Mix next four ingredients in plastic or paper bag, shaking to distribute uniformly. Put about 1/4 of the okra rounds into bag and shake. Repeat until all okra has been coated well. Fry in hot oil until brown and drain on paper towels. Best served hot.

Note: Eggplant slices or green tomato slices can be prepared in the same manner. If using eggplant, sprinkle salt over each slice before coating with meal/flour mixture; let set about 20 minutes to extract moisture and bitter flavor. If using green tomatoes, let slices soak in salty water for about 5 minutes. Drain on paper towels before coating and frying as above.

COMMANDER'S PALACE CRABMEAT IMPERIAL

❦❧❦❧❦❧❦❧❦❧❦❧❦

Long a New Orleans establishment, Commander's Palace, in the Garden District, is one more place Cap'n Andy would feel comfortable giving orders. Of the countless ways to use delectable local crabmeat, this treatment thrills all seafood lovers.

Y I E L D : 4 servings

1 pound lump crabmeat

1/2 cup scallions, finely chopped

1/2 cup green bell pepper, diced

1/4 cup pimentos, chopped

1 egg yolk (optional)

1 teaspoon dry mustard

4 artichoke hearts or 1 tablespoon capers

2 tablespoons paprika

1 cup mayonnaise (can be reduced-fat)

1/4 cup seasoned bread crumbs

1/4 cup Parmesan cheese, freshly grated

Note: Crawfish tails can be substituted or mixed with the crabmeat. With such a rich entrée, a bland side dish such as potatoes or rice goes nicely.

Health Tip: Fat can be reduced by using 1/2 cup mayonnaise and adding 1 teaspoon lemon juice (or more, to taste).

In a large bowl, combine the crabmeat, scallions, bell pepper, pimento, egg yolk, dry mustard, artichoke hearts, paprika, and 1/2 cup mayonnaise. Mix well. Season to taste. Spoon mixture into four 1-cup baking dishes, then cover with remaining mayonnaise. Sprinkle with bread crumbs and Parmesan cheese and bake at 375°F. for 15 to 20 minutes, or until heated through. Serve hot with a green salad and hot bread.

CHEF GERTRUDE PAYNE'S CRAWFISH ÉTOUFFÉE

If the argument about the pronunciation of "crawfish" can't be resolved, serve shrimp. Natives say "craw," not "cray."

Y I E L D : 8 to 10 servings

1 cup (2 sticks) butter

1/4 cup all-purpose flour

1 cup yellow onion, chopped

1 cup green onions, chopped

1/4 cup green bell pepper, chopped

1/2 cup celery, chopped

1/2 teaspoon dried basil or 1 tablespoon fresh

1 teaspoon favorite seasoned salt or herb mixture

1 teaspoon salt

1/4 cup tomato sauce

1 teaspoon Worcestershire sauce

Tabasco to taste

2 cups chicken broth

2 pounds crawfish or shrimp, peeled

1 tablespoon lemon juice

1/4 cup minced parsley

Make a dark roux by browning 1/2 cup (1 stick) butter and flour. Stir constantly to prevent burning. Add yellow and green onions, green pepper, celery, basil, and remaining butter. Sauté over medium flame and let cook for 25 to 30 minutes. Add remaining seasonings, tomato sauce, Worcestershire sauce, Tabasco, and chicken broth. Cook covered on low heat for 1 hour. Turn heat to lowest setting and add crawfish, lemon juice, and parsley. Cook for 5 minutes. Serve over rice.

Note: Étouffée dishes are central to the cuisine of South Louisiana and parts of other states where good seafood and a love for rich seasoning coexist. The term étoufée literally means "to smother" and refers to the long cooking period in liquid with the lid on the pot, especially after the seasoning vegetables have been sautéed.

STEVEDORES' POT ROAST OF BEEF WITH VEGETABLES

While the "fancier" people dine on more refined meals, the workmen on the river feast on a meal like this one. Occasionally, someone traveling first class sneaks down to partake of the pot roast, realizing what he's missing.

YIELD: 6 to 8 servings

Beef shoulder roast (3 to 4
    pounds)
1 teaspoon salt
1 teaspoon pepper
1 teaspoon garlic salt
2 tablespoons olive oil or
    vegetable oil
1/2 cup cup red wine
3/4 cup strong black brewed
    coffee

1 cup water
1/2 cup all-purpose flour
Handful fresh parsley
1 clove garlic, minced
1 large white onion, diced
1 green or red bell pepper,
    diced
2 large carrots, peeled and
    sliced into 2 inch sticks

Sprinkle meat on both sides with salt, pepper, and garlic salt. Heat oil in Dutch oven casserole with cover and brown meat on both sides. Add wine, coffee, and water (if level of liquid doesn't come almost to top of roast, add more water). Cook covered 2 hours at 300°F. Remove to meat platter.

and defat pan juices. In a large measuring cup, add 1/2 cup flour and add enough water to make 1 cup liquid; stir until smooth. Add to liquid in cooking pot, stirring. Add parsley and garlic and let gravy cook for 10 minutes. Return meat to casserole, in gravy, and add vegetables. Cover and continue to cook for 1 to 1 1/2 hours until meat and vegetables are tender. Serve on platter and arrange vegetables around meat.

ASPARAGUS or MUSHROOM RISOTTO

In the spring when asparagus is at its best, use it in risotto. Mushrooms can likewise be used to great advantage. While risotto is easy to make, it takes constant vigilance and stirring. Do not leave it to cook by itself.

YIELD: 4 to 6 servings

1 medium onion, chopped
2 tablespoons olive oil
1 cup arborio rice (no substitutes), available in many supermarkets in rice and pasta section
4 cups chicken broth, hot

12 asparagus spears, blanched or 12 large mushrooms, sliced and sautéed
1/2 cup white wine
3/4 cup Parmesan cheese, freshly grated
Pinch of saffron (optional)
Salt and pepper to taste

Sauté onion in hot olive oil, stirring until transparent. Add rice and stir to coat with oil and onion. Immediately add 1/2 cup hot broth, stirring constantly, until broth is absorbed. Add the rest of the broth by 1/2 cupfuls, stirring after each addition, until all liquid is absorbed. Add blanched asparagus or sautéed mushrooms with last addition of broth. After cooking and stirring for about 20 minutes, add white wine and continue to stir. Add grated cheese and saffron, if desired. Taste for seasoning, adding salt and pepper if needed. Serve immediately onto warm plates.

Note: If using asparagus, prepare spears as for any use. Blanch in a pot of boiling water for about 1 1/2 to 2 minutes. Cut into 1-inch lengths and add to risotto with last addition of broth. If using mushrooms, sauté mushrooms in separate skillet with 1 tablespoon butter or olive oil and add to risotto with last addition of broth. Risotto is often used as an entrée, with shrimp or sauteed prosciutto added. It is a very satisfying, rich dish, so small servings are suggested if using as a side dish.

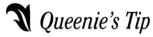

Queenie's Tip

No cook objects to being praised for a good dish.

LIZA SHARP'S CRAB AND EGGPLANT SOUP

An unusual blend of flavors, this soup is always a great hit. Divided into six larger portions and served with a salad and hot bread, this hearty soup can be an elegant supper.

YIELD: 12 servings

1 cup celery, finely chopped
1 cup onion, finely chopped
3 cups eggplant, diced
1 tablespoon olive oil
1 teaspoon dried thyme
1 teaspoon dried basil
1 teaspoon garlic, minced
1/2 cup (1 stick) butter

1/2 cup flour
2 quarts chicken or crab stock
Salt, black pepper and cayenne pepper to taste
1/2 cup cream
1 pound crabmeat

Sauté celery, onions and eggplant in olive oil until limp. Add thyme, basil and garlic and sauté 2 minutes. In another skillet, make the blond roux by heating butter and adding flour, stirring until mixture is well blended but not brown. Add to eggplant mixture and stir thoroughly. Slowly add stock and continue to cook on low heat for 15 to 20 minutes. Add seasonings. Add cream and crabmeat and serve.

ROUX

Keep ready-made roux in the refrigerator for future use. It saves time when making gravies and gumbos.

Y I E L D : 1½ cups

1 cup vegetable oil
1 cup all-purpose flour

Stir oil and flour together in a heavy skillet over low heat. Continue stirring until roux is very brown (about 30 to 45 minutes). Store tightly closed in refrigerator. For use in a recipe, mix 1 tablespoon roux into each cup of hot liquid called for. Mix thoroughly and incorporate with gumbo or gravy.

CREOLE SHRIMP GUMBO
(with Fluffy Rice)

Perhaps no other dish represents Creole cuisine to the extent that shrimp gumbo does. People from all backgrounds expect to enjoy this entrée when visiting the South. Using the roux that is native to French and Creole dishes, a cook can veer toward most seafood, fowl, or wild game (particularly duck and goose) and create a satisfying meal. Like the chowder of New England, gumbo historically has represented the "catch of the day." Another reason for the popularity of gumbo is its use of okra; in this dish the texture and flavor of this Southern vegetable weave their magic.

Y I E L D : 6 servings

6 tablespoons bacon drippings or vegetable oil
6 tablespoons flour
1½ cups onion, chopped
1 large green bell pepper, diced
2 cloves garlic, minced
3 cups seafood stock or water

1 14-ounce can stewed tomatoes
2 pounds raw shrimp, peeled
1½ pounds okra, raw and cut into "dimes"
½ cup fresh parsley, chopped
Dash Tabasco
Salt and pepper to taste

In a large skillet, heat oil and add flour, stirring over low heat until roux is very brown. Stir constantly to prevent burning (about 30 to 45 minutes). (This step is essential; the browned roux gives the gumbo its distinctive flavor.) Add onions and cook until transparent; add bell pepper and garlic, continuing to stir over low heat.

Add stock (or water) and stir until mixture thickens and resembles a dark gravy. Add tomatoes and 2 more cups water. Cook for about 15 minutes, until boiling thoroughly. Add raw shrimp and cook slowly for another 15 minutes. Add okra and seasonings and cook 20 minutes. Correct seasonings and simmer 15 minutes.

Note: Gumbo is better the second day; it is a good dish to make in advance to permit "ripening" of seasonings. Some cooks add chicken, crab, and sausage to the mixture. Serve over rice as entrée or in a small bowl as a first course.

FLUFFY RICE

No Creole cook could be forgiven for serving sticky rice. Each grain must be separate. Because rice grows in the Delta and it is a staple on tables, one must prepare it properly.

Y I E L D : 6 servings

1 cup long-grain rice
Water, enough to cover rice by 1 inch
1 tablespoon butter (or olive oil)
1 teaspoon salt

In saucepan, cover rice with water. Add butter and salt, and let water come to a boil. (If using converted rice, cover pot.) Cook on medium heat until water level is even with level of rice; cover pot, lower heat, and let rice steam for about 15 minutes. Serve hot.

QUEENIE'S ON-THE-BACK-BURNER RED BEANS AND RICE DINNER

Although she has a daily menu to adhere to, Queenie is never without a pot of red beans at hand. Called, "the poor man's meat," beans—red, white or black—can fill up a hungry deck hand very satisfactorily, quickly and economically. Served on a bed of fluffy white rice, the beans need only corn bread, sliced tomatoes and onions for a satisfying supper. Queenie gave this secret to Magnolia when she married Gaylord.

Y I E L D : 6 to 8 servings

1/4 cup bacon drippings or
    light olive oil
1 cup white or purple onion,
    chopped
1 cup celery, chopped
1 green bell pepper, chopped
2 cloves garlic, minced
2 bunches green onions,
    chopped

1 pound dried red beans (or
    white Navy or black
    beans)
1 ham bone with meat or
    2 thick slices slab bacon
1/2 teaspoon hot sauce or to
    taste
Salt and pepper to taste
White or purple onion,
    chopped for garnish

In soup pot or large Dutch oven, heat oil and sauté white or purple onions until clear. Add celery and green pepper and sauté for 3 minutes, stirring to avoid sticking. Add garlic and green onions and sauté for 3 more minutes. Add beans and ham bone or bacon and mix with sautéed vegetables. Cover beans with water, approximately 6 cups, or until water level is 3 inches above level of beans. Add seasonings. Lower heat and cover pot. Cook for approximately 2 hours. (Cooking time can be reduced to about 1 hour by soaking beans in clear water overnight.) Check for tenderness and proper seasoning. Serve beans over Fluffy Rice *(see previous page)* and pass chopped onion and extra hot sauce. Black beans can take extra condiments such as sour cream, salsa, cheese and chopped green or red bell pepper.

PORT HUDSON MACARONI AND CHEESE

❦❧❦❧❦❧❦❧❦❧❦❧❦❧❦❧❦

As a side dish or a one-dish meal, macaroni and cheese is popular on the river—the cast and crew enjoy the richness of the noodles with the sharpness of the cheese. As the boat steams out of Baton Rouge, Queenie starts supper and has it ready by the time they get to Port Hudson. Sometimes a few members of the cast are too nervous to eat before the performance, so this dish makes for a good "After the Show" Dinner. (Parthy likes to serve it because it is so economical!)

Y I E L D : Approximately 6 servings

1½ cups elbow macaroni	1½ cups cheddar cheese, grated
2 tablespoons butter	
2 tablespoons flour	Salt and pepper to taste
1 to 1½ cups milk (whole or 2%)	Sprinkle of nutmeg

Cook macaroni according to package directions, leaving noodles slightly "underdone." Drain and set aside. Melt butter in saucepan and add flour, stirring until well mixed, cooking over low heat. Gradually add milk, whisking until well mixed. Lower heat and continue to stir or whisk to prevent lumps for about 5 to 7 minutes. Add cheese and seasonings and pour sauce over macaroni, mixing, and place in an ovenproof casserole dish. Bake in 350°F. oven for 35 to 40 minutes. Additional grated cheese can be sprinkled over top during last 10 minutes of baking time.

Note: This recipe is merely the basic one for macaroni and cheese. Freshly grated Parmesan or Romano can be used in combination with the cheddar. Also, green onions can be added to the sauce. To add white onions and/or green peppers, sauté them first in a little butter before adding to the sauce. You could also add 1 to 2 cups of ham, shrimp or chicken, but that addition almost makes a tetrazzini. For variety, Queenie sometimes sprinkles some toasted walnut or pecan pieces over the top of the dish before baking.

SPICED TOMATO COULIS

Generally speaking, a coulis is made by processing a raw fruit or vegetable until it is a purée. Often a flavoring or seasoning is added to the sauce before serving.

YIELD: 1¹/₂ cups

3 ripe tomatoes, cut into chunks

Few sprigs of fresh cilantro or basil

Salt and pepper to taste

1 clove garlic

Combine all ingredients in food processor and purée. Pass as accompaniment for frittata.

FRITTATA (with Spiced Tomato Coulis)

"After the Ball Is Over" is the perfect time to have a late, late supper or a very early breakfast. If it's New Year's Eve, chances are that an omelet will taste good. It's interesting to vary that idea a bit and serve the evening version—a frittata.

YIELD: 4 generous servings

2 tablespoons olive oil

1 white potato, peeled and thinly sliced

1 onion, diced

1 red bell pepper, diced

1 zucchini, sliced (or other vegetable)

6 eggs, separated

¹/₄ cup milk

Salt, pepper, and garlic powder to taste

3 tablespoons butter

¹/₄ cup Parmesan cheese, grated (optional)

Heat oil. Add potato. Sauté until tender and brown. Lay aside. In same pan, sauté onion, red bell pepper and zucchini until tender. Lay aside with potato. In a bowl, beat egg whites until stiff, using mixer or whisk. In another bowl, beat egg yolks until thick and yellow. Add milk and seasonings to yolks. Fold in egg whites. Melt butter in first large skillet and lay sautéed vegetables on bottom. Sprinkle with grated cheese if desired. Pour egg mixture over vegetables, and cook on top of stove on low heat for 10 minutes. Place skillet in 350°F. oven for 10 to 15 minutes.

TOMATO PUDDING

An old-fashioned treatment of canned tomatoes, this "pudding" adds an interesting taste to a winter meal when fresh tomatoes are unavailable.

Y I E L D : 4 to 6 servings

2 14-ounce cans stewed
    tomatoes, diced
1 teaspoon dried parsley
    (or 3 sprigs fresh)
2 cups plain croutons
3/4 teaspoon dark brown
    sugar
2 tablespoons melted butter

In a saucepan, simmer tomatoes, herbs, and sugar until thickened slightly (15 minutes). Place croutons in greased 1½-quart casserole. Pour melted butter over croutons; toss to coat. Pour tomato mixture over croutons and stir to mix well. Bake in 350°F. oven for 1 hour. Serve hot as accompaniment to meat, fish, or egg dishes.

Queenie's Tip

To keep raw potatoes from turning brown after being peeled, cover them with ice water until using.

JULIE'S SINGIN' THE BLUES BLUE POTATO SALAD

Everything about Julie LaVerne is extraordinary—her voice, her beauty, and her secret potato salad recipe. A blue-purple potato variety is available seasonally in gourmet shops and markets that carry organic produce; get them whenever you can, as they are such a pleasure to eat. The large ones bake the same way as white ones.

YIELD: 6 to 8 servings

2 pounds small blue potatoes (or white or red)

3/4 cup mayonnaise

1/2 cup green onions, chopped

1 tablespoon capers

Salt and pepper to taste

1 teaspoon garlic salt

Handful fresh parsley

Dash powdered mustard (optional)

Boil potatoes, unpeeled, until soft. Let cool and cut into large dice. In a separate small bowl, mix remaining ingredients and pour over potatoes. Stir gently until well mixed. Can be served warm or at room temperature.

Note: This salad can be varied by adding 1 teaspoon curry powder. Adding 1 pound of cooked shrimp to the recipe turns it into an entrée. Fresh snipped basil is another good addition.

PALMER HOUSE SPINACH SALAD WITH GORGONZOLA AND WALNUTS

❦✦❦✦❦✦❦✦❦✦❦✦❦✦❦✦❦

A special meal deserves a special salad. While living well in Chicago, Magnolia learned a few culinary secrets. After succeeding on stage, she often prepared this "citified" treat for late-night suppers.

YIELD: 6 servings

1 pound fresh spinach leaves, washed and stemmed
3/4 cup Balsamic Vinaigrette *(see right)*
3/4 cup gorgonzola cheese, crumbled
3/4 cup walnut pieces, toasted at 300°F. for 10 minutes

Tear spinach leaves into bowl and toss with vinaigrette. Add cheese and nuts; toss lightly and serve immediately.

Note: This salad is robust and can be served as an entrée quite effectively. Raisins make a good addition and would go well with Pork Tenderloin *(see page 104)*.

BALSAMIC VINAIGRETTE

YIELD: 3/4 cup

2 tablespoons balsamic vinegar
2 tablespoons white vinegar
1 teaspoon Dijon mustard
1/2 teaspoon honey or sugar
1/2 teaspoon salt
1/4 teaspoon ground pepper
1/2 cup olive oil

Combine all ingredients in a jar, cover tightly and shake well to combine thoroughly.

The *Saint Joseph*, a local trader and small boat was 175 feet long and 32 feet wide and could carry several hundred bales of cotton when fully loaded.

Chapter Nine

SWEETS AND TREATS
FROM QUEENIE'S
PANTRY—HELP WHEN
"DE MIS'RY'S COMIN'
AROUN'"

Chapter Nine

SWEETS AND TREATS FROM QUEENIE'S PANTRY—HELP WHEN "DE MIS'RY'S COMIN' AROUN'"

Throughout the South, sweets reign supreme as "comfort food;" a good dessert has the power to chase the blues away. Passengers on the Cotton Blossom *are sure to eat well and eat "sweet," thanks to Queenie's culinary skill.*

LOWER MISSISSIPPI DELTA COUNTRY CHESS PIE (pictured on left on page 124)

The term "lower Mississippi" refers to any section of the river that is south of Cairo, Illinois. Distance is measured from the Gulf of Mexico northward. "Head of Passes" and Pilottown are at 0 miles, New Orleans is at 94, and Cairo, Illinois is at mile marker 954. Chess pie originated as an easy, inexpensive dessert made from readily available farm ingredients. Through the years, it entrenched itself in daily life and now comes to the table as a classic dish, full of tradition. The cornmeal distinguishes chess pie from other custard-based pies. Some recipes call for buttermilk; others add coconut.

YIELD: 8 servings

2 cups sugar
1 tablespoon all-purpose
   flour
1/4 cup cornmeal
1/4 cup (1/2 stick) unsalted
   butter or margarine,
   melted

4 eggs, slightly beaten
1 cup milk
1/4 cup fresh lemon juice
1/4 cup grated lemon rind
1 teaspoon vanilla
1 deep-dish pie shell,
   unbaked

Combine sugar, flour, and cornmeal, stirring with a fork. Add remaining ingredients; stir until blended. Pour filling into prepared, unbaked pie shell. Bake in 350°F. oven about 45 minutes. Serve when cool.

TOPPING

1/2 cup sugar

1/2 cup all-purpose flour

1/2 cup (1 stick) butter

Combine all ingredients.

Note: If meal is casual and being served in the kitchen, it's fun for the guests to see the dessert being "unveiled."

BAYOU BROWN BAG APPLE PIE
(pictured on right on page 124)

Every theme becomes more interesting when there are variations; apple pie, no matter how traditional, can be made in countless ways. This method serves Queenie well; when she senses trouble brewing, she begins peeling apples for this treat that is high on everyone's list of favorites, especially in the fall when the fruit is at its best.

YIELD: 8 servings

3 to 4 large cooking apples, especially Granny Smith

2 tablespoons lemon juice

1/2 to 3/4 cup sugar

2 tablespoons flour

1/2 teaspoon nutmeg

2 teaspoons cinnamon

1 teaspoon cloves

Dash ground ginger

1 deep-dish pie shell, unbaked

Core apples and cut into chunks (peel, if desired; not necessary). Toss with 1 teaspoon lemon juice to prevent turning brown. Combine sugar, flour, and spices; pour over apples and mix well. Transfer to pie shell and sprinkle remaining lemon juice over mixture. Combine ingredients for Topping *(at left)* and sprinkle over pie. Carefully place pie inside brown paper bag, folding the open end over two times and sealing with a paper clip. Place the bag on cookie sheet and bake in 425°F. oven for 1 hour. When done, split bag open and remove pie to serve.

"PRIDE OF THE RIVER" PECAN PIE
(with Spiked Whipped Cream)

Young cooks in the South are assured that the only way to test a pecan pie for doneness is to use a silver dinner knife—"it clings differently"—but you can make do with a toothpick. The tanginess of the spiked whipped cream balances the sweetness of the pie. Or try crème fraîche.

YIELD: 8 servings

3 eggs, slightly beaten
1 cup dark Karo corn syrup
1 cup sugar
2 tablespoons butter, melted
1 teaspoon vanilla, or more
1½ cups pecan halves
1 deep-dish pie shell, unbaked

In large bowl, mix eggs, corn syrup, sugar, melted butter, and vanilla by hand until well blended. Stir in pecans and mix well. Pour mixture into pie shell, and bake in 350°F. oven about 55 minutes, or until blade of silver dinner knife comes out clean when stuck in center of pie. Let cool before cutting. When serving, top with Spiked Whipped Cream or crème fraîche.

Note: When baking, set pie on cookie sheet in oven, as filling tends to spill over sides of pie pan until mixture thickens.

SPIKED WHIPPED CREAM

This is whipped cream for celebrations.

YIELD: About 1½ cups

1 cup whipping cream
2 tablespoons bourbon or 1 tablespoon brandy
1 teaspoon vanilla

Whip cream. Just as soft peaks form, add flavorings. Whip again just until peaks become slightly stiff.

Queenie's Tip

I never met a man who didn't like chocolate cake.

DOWNRIVER CHOCOLATE CAKE
(with Coffee-tinged Fudge-Pecan Frosting)

No dessert collection would be complete without something chocolate. This cake, known in some towns on the river as "The Only Cake There Is," satisfies cast, crew, and any drop-in visitors to the Cotton Blossom.

YIELD: 1 large sheet cake or 2 layers

2 cups all-purpose flour

2 cups sugar

$1/2$ teaspoon salt

$1/2$ cup (1 stick) butter or margarine

1 cup water

$1/2$ cup cooking oil

6 rounded tablespoons cocoa powder

2 teaspoons instant coffee granules

1 teaspoon baking soda

$1/2$ cup buttermilk

2 eggs

2 teaspoons vanilla

Preheat oven to 350°F. Mix together flour, sugar, and salt, and set aside. In a saucepan, melt butter and add water, oil, cocoa powder, and instant coffee granules. Heat just until boiling. Pour over flour mixture and mix well. Add soda to buttermilk and stir into chocolate mixture. Beat eggs with vanilla and add to chocolate mixture. Pour into greased sheet cake pan (or 2 square layer cake pans). Bake in 350°F. oven for 20 to 25 minutes. Frost cake *immediately* when it comes out of the oven.

COFFEE-TINGED FUDGE-PECAN FROSTING

Y I E L D : About 2^1/$_2$ cups,
    enough to frost 2 layers
    or one sheet cake

^{1}/$_2$ cup (1 stick) butter or
    margarine
6 tablespoons evaporated
    milk, plus a bit more
6 rounded tablespoons cocoa
    powder
2 teaspoons instant coffee
    granules
1 16-ounce box confectioners'
    sugar
2 teaspoons vanilla
1 cup pecans pieces or halves

Place all ingredients in skillet and heat over low flame just until butter
melts and mixture can be stirred easily; take off heat, stir, and pour over
hot cake *immediately* upon removing cake from oven.

Note: This cake can be frozen; it makes a great dessert when a small
piece is paired with vanilla ice cream and a purée of fresh or frozen
raspberries.

MAMA'S WORLD-CLASS, NONE-BETTER NEW ORLEANS CREOLE PRALINES

Most travelers to the Crescent City never get to know a truly good praline, as they buy the candy in "tourist trap" stores. Residents of New Orleans either make the pralines themselves or have a secret source, in someone's home, rather than a commercial one. This recipe is a very private one, taught to Queenie by her mother. Practice, in this case, really does make perfect.

Y I E L D : Approximately 2 dozen 2½" pralines

2 cups sugar	2 cups pecan halves
1 cup buttermilk	1 tablespoon butter
1 teaspoon baking soda	2 teaspoons vanilla

Note: For tea or to conclude any special occasion, an antique plate or silver tray, laden with pralines, is placed on the sideboard. Sometimes the candies are passed, like after-dinner mints, after dessert!

In a large saucepan, bring sugar and buttermilk to a boil. Add soda slowly (otherwise the mixture tends to boil over), and cook until a soft ball forms in a cup of cool water. (Time to come to the soft ball stage varies; after about 7 minutes of stirring, drop about a teaspoon of mixture in water and rub it between fingers; when ball is about to form, difference is evident. This step is crucial. Or use a candy thermometer, which has a "soft ball stage" on it.) When soft ball stage is reached, remove pan from heat and add pecans, butter, and vanilla. Beat candy with large spoon until it is thick enough to drop by spoonfuls onto waxed paper (mixture will look less glossy when it is ready to spoon).

"COTTON BLOSSOMS" (Meringue Cookies—pictured on page 68)

Egg whites are used to create light confections the world over; their versatility makes them essential in soufflés, cakes, and meringues. Queenie's meringue cookies pair with some fresh strawberries at afternoon tea. She always puts a few aside for Joe to have after supper, as he likes them so much.

Y I E L D : About 2 dozen cookies

4 egg whites from extra-large or jumbo eggs

1/2 teaspoon salt

1 cup sugar

1 teaspoon white vinegar (or 1/4 teaspoon cream of tartar)

1 1/2 to 2 teaspoons vanilla

Preheat oven to 450°F. Line baking sheet with waxed paper and lightly oil paper. With mixer on high speed, beat egg whites with salt until soft peaks form. Add sugar 1 tablespoon at a time, beating after each addition, until stiff peaks form. Fold in vinegar and vanilla, and mix gently. Drop batter gently from spoon onto paper. Place baking sheet into oven, immediately reducing heat to lowest setting (no more than 250°F.). Bake 1 1/4 hours. Turn off oven and leave "Cotton Blossoms" in oven until cool. Serve or store immediately in airtight tins.

Note: Toasted pecan pieces or chocolate bits can be added to make a variety of meringue types. Never leave these cookies unstored for long; the slightest bit of humidity makes them limp and inedible. Never refrigerate, for the same reason.

Health Tip: These "Blossoms" have 0 fat calories, and they are heart healthy! Sugar can be reduced to 1/2 cup.

CAP'N AND MRS. HAWKES' CELEBRATION HOMEMADE ICE CREAM

꧁ ꧂ ꧁ ꧂ ꧁ ꧂ ꧁ ꧂ ꧁ ꧂ ꧁ ꧂

Note: 1½ cups puréed fruit or 2 ounces melted semisweet chocolate may be added to the custard before freezing.

At the end of a show's run, the cast and crew must pack quickly in order to get to their next engagement. With little leisure before or after a performance, all hands are ready for a little celebration, a ritual that implies a reward for a job well done. After they're on the river, Cap'n Andy cranks up the ice cream freezer as a way of thanking the "team members." Sitting down together while devouring the rich ice cream reestablishes everyone's love for show business on a "floating palace theatre."

YIELD: 2 quarts of ice cream

6 egg yolks

2 cups milk

1 cup sugar

⅓ teaspoon salt

2½ tablespoons vanilla

2 cups whipping cream
  (unwhipped)

In a mixing bowl, whisk egg yolks until mixed well. Add milk and whisk until well blended. In top of a double boiler, stir in sugar and salt. Cook over simmering, but not boiling, water, whisking constantly, until sauce coats the back of a metal spoon (about 10 to 15 minutes). Cool, cover and chill in refrigerator. Stir in vanilla and cream when mixture is cold. Freeze according to directions on ice cream freezer. (If an old-fashioned hand-crank freezer is used, the process takes about 30 minutes). Top with Praline Sauce *(see opposite page).*

CAMELLIA-BORDERED VERANDA PRALINE SAUCE

Queenie brings out this praline sauce for the ice cream.

YIELD: About 2½ cups

2 cups ribbon cane syrup or dark Karo syrup

⅓ cup boiling water

⅓ cup brown sugar

1 cup pecan halves or chopped pieces

1 teaspoon vanilla

2 tablespoons butter

Combine all ingredients except the butter in saucepan and cook over medium heat just until mixture comes to a boil. Remove from heat, stir in butter, and serve like hot fudge sauce or let cool before using. Keeps indefinitely in a tightly-sealed jar. Good as a gift item.

MISSISSIPPI GRIS GRIS AND LOUISIANA LAGNIAPPE

Wherever voodoo has been practiced, the word "gris gris" (pronounced "gree gree") has followed close behind. At Mardi Gras, some celebrants wear pouches on their costumes that contain powder with alleged special properties—either the power to cast spells or bring bad or good luck. In common usage, gris gris refers to paraphernalia of all kinds, as in "Why do you always leave your gris gris at my house?"

Although Cap'n Andy believes in giving everybody "just a sample," he usually winds up, as Parthy often reminds him, "givin' away the whole show for nuthin'." This attitude defines "lagniappe" ("lan-yap"), which means giving a little something beyond what is required. Although the term comes from French settlers, the attitude abounds in the South today. We want our guests to take away just a little more than what is expected. Lagniappe—that's what the following recipes are. They are not required, but they add a special zest to a meal. Cap'n Andy's overly generous nature lives on in Show Boat: the songs are prettier, the sets more elaborate, and the joy more lasting.

PEPPER-FLAVORED OIL

This condiment can be added to salad dressings or used in a sauté pan when oil is called for. Use sparingly, as the flavor is quite strong after two weeks.

Fill a pint jar loosely with fresh hot peppers of choice (green chilies, jalapeño, etc.) mixing red and green colors for eye appeal. Fill jar with light olive oil that has been heated but not boiled and seal for about one week before using. Keeps for about 6 weeks.

Note: Other ingredients can be added for extra flavors. Some suggestions are the following: peppercorns—black or multi-colored; onion slices; sprigs of rosemary, basil or herbs of choice.

PEPPER-FLAVORED VINEGAR

Used wherever vinegar is used for flavor, this mixture definitely adds zest; use sparingly.

Repeat process for flavored oil, using white wine vinegar (or a ½ and ½ mixture of red wine and white wine vinegar) and peppers of choice. Heat vinegar, but do not boil, before pouring over peppers. Seal in jars.

QUEENIE'S BALLY-HOO SPICED PEACHES

In the summer, sometimes there are just too many ripe peaches; Queenie uses the surplus to make pickled peaches to savor in the fall and winter—a good item for Queenie's pantry shelf. The term "bally-hoo" has sometimes been misinterpreted to mean "clap trap" or "baloney." Actually the term refers to a sales pitch, much like the "pitch" delivered by a barker at a circus. Its purpose is to drum up business.

YIELD: 1 dozen spiced peaches

1 dozen large peaches
1 cup sugar
1 pint vinegar, diluted with ½ cup water
5 cinnamon sticks
1 tablespoon whole cloves
1 tablespoon whole allspice

Peel peaches and place in a jar or earthenware container with lid. Boil next five ingredients together for about 10 minutes. Pour hot syrup over fruit and leave for 24 hours. On the following day, drain syrup off fruit, boil and pour hot syrup over fruit again. Repeat process every day for 10 days. On eleventh day, boil syrup once again, put fruit in jars with cinnamon sticks, and pour hot liquid over peaches. Seal jars.

Queenie's Tip

Southern food doesn't have to be
fancy; it does have to be fresh.

JULIE'S CORN RELISH

When Julie left the cast of the Cotton Blossom, *she passed this recipe on to Magnolia, who then shared it with Queenie so that the potluck dinners could continue with this favorite condiment. Not only a good condiment for a potluck, Julie's relish makes good gifts and can be made spicier with the addition of jalapeño peppers, if desired.*

Y I E L D : 6 cups

1 tablespoon cornstarch	1 large cucumber, peeled and diced
1 teaspoon turmeric	3 cups fresh corn
1 cup white or cider vinegar	4 stalks celery, diced
2 green bell peppers, seeded and diced	1$1/4$ cups sugar
2 red peppers, seeded and diced	1 teaspoon mustard seeds
	Dash curry powder

In large pot, blend cornstarch and tumeric with 1 tablespoon of the vinegar. Add the rest of the vinegar, and mix in remaining ingredients. Bring to boil, then lower heat, simmering slowly for 1 hour. Pour into hot jars (sterilized by running through dishwasher cycle) and seal.

PARTHY'S HOMEMADE BREAD-AND-BUTTER PICKLES

In some small towns, selected cooks are known for certain recipes, and people along the river said about Parthy, "You ought to try her pickles!"

YIELD: 8 pints

8 pounds pickling cucumbers

6 medium onions, white and purple, sliced

2 green peppers, sliced

4 cloves garlic

1/3 cup sea salt, coarse grind

5 cups sugar

1 1/2 teaspoons turmeric

1 1/2 teaspoons celery seed

3 tablespoons mustard seed

3 cups cider vinegar

Leave skin on cucumber and slice thinly. Add onions, peppers, whole garlic cloves and salt. Mix in 6 cups cracked ice or ice cubes. Let stand 3 hours and drain well. In a large kettle, combine all other ingredients. Add cucumber mixture and heat just to boiling point. Seal in hot jars (sterilized by running through dishwasher cycle).

Note: Like the corn relish, these pickles make good gifts. A tasty variation of this recipe can be achieved by adding a tablespoon of curry powder to the heated solution.

BLACKBERRY JAM

Few people who have seen fresh blackberry jam oozing onto a hot buttered biscuit can forget the sight. Queenie saves some jam for holiday gift-giving, as everyone up and down the river looks forward to the treat. Her secret formula: equal parts of sugar and berries.

Y I E L D : Approximately
    3 cups

4 cups blackberries

4 cups sugar

Wash berries and remove any damaged ones. Pour sugar over berries and set aside to let them "juice" for 20 minutes. Cook berry mixture in a heavy pot and bring to a boil over medium heat. Cook over very low heat for about 20 minutes or until mixture has thickened. (Be careful not to scorch mixture; stir frequently.) Seal in decorative jars for gift-giving.

FIG PRESERVES

During the summer when figs are plentiful, the cast and crew help Queenie gather them on all their stops. They know she will turn them into her peerless fig preserves for winter use. Some of the figs appear on the supper sideboard, but Parthy watches carefully to see that they get saved for cooking.

Y I E L D : Approximately 16 pints

16 pounds figs

$1/2$ cup baking soda

12 pounds sugar

2 lemons, sliced

Wash figs and sprinkle $1/2$ cup baking soda over them. Cover with boiling water and let stand 2 or 3 minutes. Drain and rinse several times. Add sugar to drained figs and cook until mixture comes to a rolling boil. Lower heat and cook until clear (about 30 or 40 minutes). Add two lemons, sliced. Transfer figs into another pan and continue cooking syrup until it is very thick. Put figs back into syrup and let stand until cool. Reheat and pour preserves into hot, sterilized jars.

Note: For cooks with a fig tree close at hand, two gallons of figs are easy to obtain. For others less fortunate, buy figs in smaller quantity and keep to the proportions suggested above, reducing baking soda proportionally. Use fig preserves as topping for ice cream. A spot of brandy goes well in the mixture.

DELTA QUEEN CAJUN SPICE

Chef Paul Wayland-Smith and many good cooks have made up concoctions—gris gris—that they consider all-purpose dry seasoning mixtures; they rub the spicy powder on meat, put it in salad dressings and rice dishes and sprinkle it over fish and seafood. Queenie keeps hers in a jar on a shelf near the stove so that she doesn't have to search it out when she needs it. On the rivers and bayous, the mixtures always contain some cayenne pepper.

Y I E L D : Approximately 5 cups

1/4 cup oregano (dried)	2 tablepoons cayenne pepper
1/2 cup thyme (dried)	2 tablepoons white pepper
1/4 cup basil (dried)	3/4 cup salt
1/2 cup garlic powder	11/4 cups paprika
3/4 cup onion powder	
1/4 cup black pepper	

Combine all ingredients in a large jar with a tight lid. Use when some "cooking magic" is needed.

Note: As executive chef of the The Delta Queen Steamboat Co., Paul Wayland-Smith needs large quantities of spices; the home cook may want to halve the recipe.

CAJUN BEURRE BLANC

This recipe also comes from Chef Paul Wayland-Smith of The Delta Queen Steamboat Co.

Y I E L D : Approximately 5 cups

1 cup white wine
1/4 cup lemon juice
1/4 teaspoon black peppercorns, ground
1/2 tablespoon shallots, chopped
1/2 bay leaf, crushed
1/2 cup whipping cream
21/2 cups butter
1/2 cup Cajun Spice *(at left)*

Reduce white wine, lemon juice, pepper, shallots, and bay leaf to a syrup. Add cream and reduce to syrup again. Fold in butter in chunks, whisking until smooth. Put sauce through fine sieve strainer. Serve with roasted meats or grilled fish.

HOW TO SPEAK "RIVER"

The beauty and majesty of the Mississippi River have inspired the imaginations of artists and writers for many years. In addition to Edna Ferber's novel, Show Boat, *and its magnificent musical adaptation by Jerome Kern and Oscar Hammerstein II, Mark Twain introduced the world to this culture, especially expressions used on the river. Some of them have become a part of everyday speech in the South. For other phrases, a glossary is necessary. Perhaps the best way to learn to speak "River," is to take a trip along the Mississippi and hear the language firsthand. Seeing the country from a paddlewheeler teaches us what Twain felt when he expressed his love for* "Life on the Mississippi."

ABOVE, The tow boat *J. B. O'Brien,* built in 1878, was a part of the Natchez riverfront scene for more than 20 years.

BELVEDERE: A walkway built on the roof of plantation houses to permit observation of river traffic and the arrival of guests by boat. Called a "Widow's Walk" in coastal New England.

BUCKET BOARDS: The bucket planks of the paddlewheel that dip into the water as the wheel turns.

CAIRO, ILLINOIS: The town where the Mississippi and Ohio meet; officially the end of the lower Mississippi and beginning of the upper Mississippi.

Named after the city in Egypt, but pronounced "Kay-row," it was a bustling riverboat town a hundred years ago (mile marker 954).

CABIN, MAIN CABIN, OR SALOON: Used as lobby, lounge, dining room, and entertainment hall, the main cabin ran the full length of a steamboat, with passenger staterooms opening off it. On a boat like the famous *J. M. White,* the cabin was 233 feet long, 19 feet wide with a 13-foot ceiling.

CHOKIN' A STUMP: Pulling into the river bank and tying up to a tree. A favorite method for weathering a fog.

CROSSING: Used as a noun, it indicates the place to move from one side of the river to the other, to gain "slack water," thus minimizing the fight against the river's powerful current.

RIGHT, Mule-drawn wagons transported the bales of cotton to the river landings for transfer to the steamboats.

CHALMETTE: Location on the river south of New Orleans, where Andrew Jackson and the "Pirate Patriot" Jean Lafitte defeated the British in the Battle of New Orleans.

DELTA: Area on lower Mississippi River, especially south of Memphis, where richness of the soil led to fortunes in sugar cane and cotton crops. In its course southward, the river deposits some 356,000 tons of sediment daily, and the Delta has been formed from that buildup. Toward the Gulf of Mexico, the land is marshy and basically unchanged since 1682, when Sieur de La Salle and his band first traveled to the mouth of the river to claim the land for France.

FLOATING THEATER: A phenomenon on the major rivers, dating from about 1817 through 1920 or a little later. These were not self-powered boats, but pushed by a small steamboat (ironically referred to as a "tow boat"). In her novel, Edna Ferber described the show boat as "a flat-bottomed barge that looked like a house sitting on the river." These boats went up and down waterways, calling two times a year on towns on the banks of the rivers, performing musical shows and melodramas.

LEVEE: A man-made embankment ten to fifteen feet high along the lower Mississippi, built to prevent flooding of low-lying areas during periods of high water.

LOADED TO THE GUARDS: An expression that described a steamer fully loaded with bales of cotton and other cargo. In 1875, a steamboat captain wrote, "the cotton is 12 tiers high on our guards. If our passengers get a peep of daylight they have to go to the hurricane deck or in the pilothouse."

MARK TWAIN: Every school child used to know that Mark Twain was the *nom de plume* of the American humorist Samuel Clemens of Hannibal, Missouri. On the river, the term indicates the water's depth. A leadsman worked on the bow of the steamboat, throwing a line marked to indicate various depths. He called the results to the pilot, who then knew how to better steer the boat. "Mark Twain" indicated a depth of 12 feet—safe passage for the vessel's draft.

NATCHEZ: Named after the Natchez Indians, it marks the termination of the famed Natchez Trace. Natchez is the home of Fort Rosalie, site of the struggle between the government and Native Americans in the early nineteenth century. The Natchez Pilgrimage in spring and fall features many antebellum homes and gardens open to visitors.

OAK ALLEY: A plantation in Vacherie, Louisiana, upriver from New Orleans. A present-day stop for tourist boats, open to the public. (Recently used as setting for the movie *Interview with a Vampire*.)

PACKET: A vessel that carried a combination of cargo and passengers. Today's commercial steamboats on the Mississippi carry only passengers.

PATTING HER FEET: A barge moving along nicely.

PILOTTOWN: Going north, a settlement at mile marker 0, where ocean pilots and river pilots trade duties.

PITMAN ARM: The shaft that turns the paddlewheel on a steamboat.

RIVER MILES: Speed on rivers is measured in miles, not knots. In terms of distance, mile markers are placed on the river, starting at 0 at the mouth at the Gulf of Mexico and continuing to Cairo, Illinois, at marker 954. From there begins marker 0 for the upper Mississippi, thus ending the lower Mississippi.

ROSEDOWN: A plantation with 28 acres of gardens in St. Francisville, Louisiana, another stop on the upriver trip to Natchez. Open to the public.

STAGE: The gangway of a steamboat, hoisted out front while boat is moving. Sometimes the crew used the space to put on shows for townspeople while docked. When boat is in motion, it is called a "swinging stage."

STATEROOM: Rooms on steamboats were not numbered, but, rather, identified with the names of states.

TEXAS DECK: The third deck on a steamboat, originally used for officers' quarters. River historian Capt. Fred Way explains that this term is used because Texas was admitted to the Union in 1845, about the same time this deck became common on steamboats.

TRADE: A noun, used to describe the regular route of a steamboat packet, as in the St. Louis-New Orleans trade.

VICKSBURG: Another Mississippi stop on the steamboat's northward journey, between Natchez and Greenville. Scene of a bloody Civil War battle and the National Military Park to commemorate the action. Also of interest to Civil War buffs is the exhibit of the *U.S.S. Cairo,* the ironclad that sank, was preserved in the river's mud, and then was salvaged in 1964.

LEFT, The landing at Natchez-Under-the-Hill with the swollen Mississippi River swallowing many water front buildings.

Index